The Greatest Enemy Is YOU

Tim Chang

iUniverse, Inc.
New York   Bloomington

The Greatest Enemy is You!
Personal Finance

Copyright © 2010 Tim Chang

iUniverse books may be ordered through booksellers or by contacting:

iUniverse
1663 Liberty Drive
Bloomington, IN 47403
www.iuniverse.com
1-800-Authors (1-800-288-4677)

ISBN: 978-1-4502-4791-7 (pbk)
ISBN: 978-1-4502-4793-1 (ebk)

Printed in the United States of America

iUniverse rev. date: 9/24/2010

Message from the Author

I believe that the majority of society's woes, such as crime, family break-downs, and health issues, are mainly caused by money problems. For this reason I am dedicated to teaching people how money works. If people are able to keep more of their money and successfully manage their finances, they can prevent a lot of financial stress. And having less stress enables people to lead happier, healthier lives.

I'm passionate about coaching clients so they can understand and recognize the factors that keep them from achieving their financial goals. For example, banks, insurance companies, and tax agencies often leave clients in the dark, at their clients' expense. They charge for substandard service and withhold information about more cost-effective strategies from thousands of unsuspecting customers. I want to help people better manage their relationships with bankers, insurers, and taxmen so they can keep more money for themselves.

Think of me as your money coach. I'm here to alleviate the financial challenges facing most North Americans, who are struggling in one of the richest continents in the world. But the reality is 5% of the world population owns 90% of the wealth, leaving the remaining 95% with only 10%. This is not by accident, social engineering through government design, or the "Almighty" God. The biggest thing holding you back is you. This book contains articles that provide most of the answers for the majority of 95% who aspire to join the top 5%. Through this book I hope to empower people to take control of their personal finances and make their money work for them, rather than for banks, insurance companies and tax agencies.

Tim Chang
FCMA (UK), CPM,CMA,CFP®

Do I Need Help with my Financial Planning?

A quiz by the Financial Planners Standards Council to determine the value of working with a financial advisor. For each question answer 'Agree,' 'Disagree,' or 'Not Sure.'

1. "I understand the tax implications of my decisions. I pay a lot of tax. "

2. "I sleep well at night knowing my money is working as hard as I am."

3. "Insurance? Yeah, I understand it – sort of."

4. "How hard can it be? I've got the time and skills to put my own financial plan together."

5. "I have money saved for what I know and don't know will happen."

6. "I know there is a difference between good debt and bad debt."

7. "I know what my financial legacy will – or must be."

8. "Retirement? Absolutely. Just don't ask me when or how."

9. "I know the precise value of what I own."

10. "Maybe I could use a little help from a professional financial planner."

Introduction

North Americans are on the brink of a retirement crisis. Due to years of avoiding talk about the future, and not planning accordingly, 75% of Canadians have no defined pension plan – that is, no guaranteed retirement income – and the situation is just as grim in the United States of America. We are already seeing the effects of our, and a number of institutions', lack of planning, and current events will only add to the strain. Even though the first group of baby boomers is only expected to retire in 2012, increased health care needs have added another burden to the financial health of each and every one of us in Canada, and with the overhauling of the health care system in the U.S. the burden will be felt along with the benefits. With our aging population, the escalating cost of health care has already taken away 45-50% of the budgets of most Canadian provinces, and because so many North Americans maintain an unhealthy lifestyle the numbers are only likely to rise. So what does that mean for retirement? North Americans may not be able to rely on the government for a steady pension. Already the public pension and welfare payments offered by the Canadian and American governments make it nearly impossible to live comfortably; imagine how further strained budgets might exacerbate the situation. We need to take retirement savings into our own hands.

It's a shame that so many people haven't understood the need for adequate savings for so long. It is difficult to determine who is at fault, because we are largely responsible for our own circumstances. But we are not the only ones culpable. The responsibility should be shouldered by four parties: Banks, Insurance companies, the Government, and the people. First let's consider each individual's role.

So many North Americans do not bother to acquire basic knowledge about personal finance. Because so few adequately understand how money works, saving for retirement is not made a priority. So often we get caught up in the present and neglect to think about the future. But giving some thought to the future now will make retirement a lot more comfortable. Everyone deserves to lead life with dignity. That's true for the youth of the nation as much as it is for the elderly. Now that we are starting to see some of the consequences of financial naivety, we must take measures to educate future generations. If we are to prevent financial crises, personal finance must become a mandatory course in high school, college, and university. We must also take the time to educate ourselves and our loved ones.

Of course, this is no easy task when the financial institutions we trust lead us astray. Banks are another guilty party, as they engage in gauging and they misuse the trust placed in them by the government and the public. There is an abominable lack of transparency and standardization in legal documentation. Banks are not upfront about the cost of breaking a mortgage, for example. When interest rates are low many homeowners are encouraged to break a fixed mortgage to improve cash flow; but when you calculate the administration and break fees this option could be just as expensive as sticking to the original terms. The true cost of credit cards and carrying credit card debt is not explained. The details are so buried in the fine print that one would have to be a lawyer to do some digging and understand all of the details of these documents. Banks are also infamous for promoting GICs, term deposits, and checking accounts, often using fear tactics and almost always charging exorbitant fees. The interest returns on 'safe' investments hardly match the rate of inflation. Perhaps worst of all, resources are so unequal between financial institutions and the public that those who might want to enforce legal rights are discouraged from even trying. The essential question is, "How can ordinary people win the money game against banks and insurers?" Put bluntly, "How can an amateur hockey player win against NHL players?" The difference is too great.

Insurance Companies share a lot of the banks' abuses. There is a lack of transparency and a lack of standardization in legal documentation; products that are not suitable for clients are sold simply because they are more profitable for the company; and insurance companies tout investment products with returns that might be worse than GICs and term deposits, once management fees are factored in.

Finally, the Government, at both the Federal and Provincial/State levels, is responsible. The present tax and welfare system encourages an underground economy, which makes fair distribution of the tax burden and social benefits impossible. This puts a disproportionate burden on honest, hardworking taxpayers. To put a halt to the abuses of Banks and Insurance Companies, Government regulators should enforce standard legal documentation for various products offered by these institutions. Lobbying by these institutions should also be outlawed; they are so powerful that no politician in power dares to put an end to their greed, so their greed is permitted at the expense of ordinary folks. To solve the problem of inadequate representation, a "Financial Arbitration Centre" with regional offices should be created to provide a quick and inexpensive way for clients to bring complaints of the abuses they suffered at the hands of Financial Institutions; the present court system is too bureaucratic and too expensive for ordinary North Americans. In Canada, unfortunately these reforms are unlikely to occur under the present minority government, and it seem this minority status will be a permanent feature in Canadian Parliament given that smaller parties, like the Bloc Québécois, which are unlikely to become the governing party, take away a substantial number of seats from bigger contenders.

Although there is little we can do about larger organizations, we can do work on the individual level. I've assembled this collection of essays because the more knowledgeable you are about where your money goes, the better you can take control of your financial future. I will discuss the issues listed above in the three sections of this book: Your Money, Your Business, and Your Future.

In "Your Money" you will find a number of articles explaining the nature of your relationships with your bank, the tax agency, and yourself. I set the facts straight about the costs of real estate, and some of the misconceptions many people have about borrowing through a mortgage and paying it off early. When you understand what's really happening to your money you can make wiser decisions. Rather than following the advice of friends and neighbours, who may be just as uncertain as you are about financial decisions, you'll learn where to turn for advice and money management. Once you know how to better manage your relationships with bankers, insurers, and taxmen you can keep more money for yourself.

The second section is entitled "Your Future," though perhaps it should be "Your Life" or "Your Family." This is because many of the articles in this section discuss your retirement goals, and retirement planning has an enormous impact on the quality of your life and on the lives of your loved ones. You will also find articles about trusts and estate planning, your legacy, and general insurance. It can be difficult to think about the future, but this is where financial planning is most important. It's impossible to predict the future, but intelligent financial planning can help you prepare for what life has in store.

The third, and last, section – "Your Business" – is a section dedicated to business owners (and entrepreneurs who need to know the ropes). This section includes articles about everything from starting up to succession planning. Inside you'll find some information about tax deductions and partnerships. Read the articles that most interest you and that you feel apply to your unique situation. And of course, if you have any other questions you can contact me.

I hope that you will find these articles helpful. My aim is to educate, because if you are able to keep more of your money and successfully manage your finances, you can prevent a lot of financial stress. And having less stress enables you to lead a happier, healthier life.

Table of Contents

Introduction

Your Money   12

- Your Greatest Enemy is You   15
- My Rule of Thumb   19
- How Money Works   21
- Strategic Investment Planning   24
- Mastering the Bank and the Tax Agency   27
- Why Paying Down your Mortgage is Not a Sound Decision
                                                                    33
- Why Real Estate is Not a Good Investment   35
- The Potential Canadian Housing Bubble   39
- How to Avoid a Tax Audit   42
- Job Loss   44

Your Future   49

- The Role of the Financial Planner in Retirement Planning
                                                                    53
- The Golden Years   54
- Plan for a Comfortable Retirement   58
- Top 9 Retirement Savings Tips   62
- TFSA over RRSP   64
- Pre-Retirement Process   65
- Trusts and Estate Planning   67

Your Business   75

- The Challenges and Sacrifices of Business Ownership 76
- Financial Projections and Business Plans   79
- Feasibility Study   80
- Budgetary and Financial Planning For Business   82
- Guide to Setting up a New Businesses   84
- Thinking of Retail Business? Just Say "No!"   87
- Small Business Deduction   91

- Taxes on Dividends 99
- Taxable Income and Tax Payable for Corporation 108
- Maximize Your Tax Deductions 117
- Management Consultancy 127
- Partnerships 128
- Business Valuation and Buying or Selling an Incorporated Business 137
- Succession Planning 142

Tim Chang Profile 148

Your Money

Most North Americans feel some sort of financial strain. As demonstrated in the chart below, an overwhelming majority of Canadians (and Americans) worry that they won't have enough retirement savings to last the rest of their lives. Though different families' main concerns might vary, most financial issues are connected. Those who worry that they don't have enough retirement savings have the same trouble with managing their money and sticking to budgets as those who worry about debt or insufficient savings. Saving money is not made the high priority it ought to be because people haven't learned to use their money effectively. Many families have trouble paying bills, credit cards, mortgage, and car payments, so managing debt is a major concern. And because so many adults can expect to care for their children as well as their aging parents, money has to be especially well-managed in order for people to secure children's futures without neglecting themselves or their parents.

Financial Chalenges

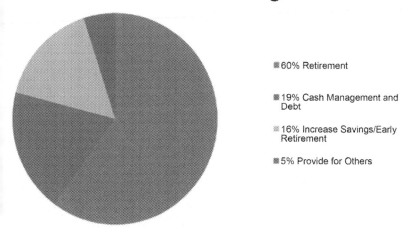

- 60% Retirement
- 19% Cash Management and Debt
- 16% Increase Savings/Early Retirement
- 5% Provide for Others

Perhaps the reason so many people feel they are falling short is because they often go against conventional wisdom. We are told to "Buy low and sell high," but so often do-it-yourself investors are unwilling to wait through the low points and think about their investments as long-term projects.

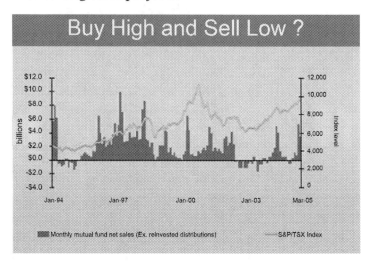

As a result, people usually end up buying high, panicking, and then selling low. They let their emotions guide their financial decisions rather than good sense and sound advice. Investments require commitment. One has to leave fears and emotions out of finance management.

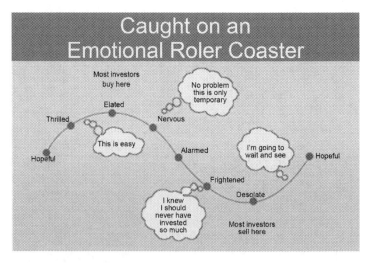

People also require financial advisors' expertise. Thanks to the advice available on the Internet it seems almost anyone can successfully manage investments, playing the stock market with ease. But although there is plenty of good advice in Internet articles, it's important to consult a trusted financial advisor before putting your money at stake. The advice given to the average do-it-yourself investor only skims the surface of all of the intricacies of financial management. There's simply too much to learn! A financial advisor is trained in all of the details you can easily miss. The proof is in the results. Do-it-yourself investors consistently underperform the markets.

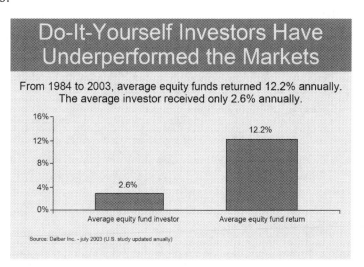

Simple mistakes like these keep people from putting their money to work for them. In this section I've included articles that will help you understand how your money is being used, and how you can use it to your advantage. But first, we have to take a look at what so many North Americans are getting wrong.

Additionally, in this section, you will find some articles about how to manage your finances when life burdens you with a heavier load, and also for times when you are financially comfortable and secure. Sometimes you will find that you need financial help, while at other points you might be able to offer financial assistance. Remember that putting your money to work for you means putting it to work for the people and organisations you care about as well.

Your Greatest Enemy is You

Sometimes the only thing holding us back from financial security is our own personality traits. Identifying destructive behaviours now can help you make changes to secure a better financial future. Read on to discover some of the most misguided assumptions we make.

The Procrastinator

Procrastination is simply the deferment of actions or tasks to a later time. Psychologists often cite such behaviour as a mechanism for coping with the anxiety associated with starting and/or completing any task or even making a decision. For a behaviour to be classified as procrastinatory, it must fulfil three criteria: it must be counterproductive, needless, and detaining.

Someone who procrastinates misses out on the benefits of compound interest. This means that if you start saving for retirement at forty-five you will have to contribute almost six times as much money each month in order to retire with the same retirement assets as someone who started saving at twenty-five. Look at this chart to see how this works.

Starting age	25	35	45
Retirement Assets @ 65; ROI = 8%	$980,000	$980,000	$980,000
Retirement Income Per year	$40,000	$40,000	$40,000
Required Investment per month	$ 300	$700	$1,700

The Know-It-All:

A relatively trouble-free trip through the education system can make any successful student susceptible to the know-it-all mentality. This attitude often stems from a high sense of self-worth due to excellent grades in school. For the know-it-all, it's always best to be right and asking for help means accepting defeat.

Financially, the know-it-all often has a lot of knowledge but takes no action. The know-it-all will spend time and energy researching various topics and subjects, but seldom puts theory into practice. You cannot build wealth if you are just a talker, and not a doer.

The Mislead Person:

There are many who believe the government will take care of them in retirement. But if you think government help will support you, think again. The Canada Pension Plan and Old Age Security are not meant to meet retirees' needs – and the situation is no better in the U.S.A. If you depend on only these resources you will live well below the poverty level.

Here are the average C.P.P. and O.A.S. benefit payments in Canada for 2009.

CPP $472.36

OAS   <u>$464.64</u>

Total Benefits $937.00 per month

The total average benefit is only $11,244 per year!

The Dreamer:

Because it was common in the past for children to take care of their parents once they retired, many believe that they will be able to put themselves into the care of their children. But in recent years it has become very common for parents to play host to their adult children. This is, in part, due to a difficult job market and high living expenses, but debilitating student loans also play a part. Another factor is that the cost of living in urban areas is significantly higher than living elsewhere. Young adults with low incomes and/or uncertain job futures might hesitate longer before renting an apartment if their parents can provide housing.

Media, television, and movies often portray this living arrangement, which is growing in popularity largely out of necessity. Such media depict the difficulties that many parents have telling their kids that it's time for them to leave the nest. In many of these scenarios, the picture drawn is one of frustrated parents enduring a situation they had neither planned nor prepared for. As is often the case, part of the popular view about adult children living at home is probably not without foundation. Some parents might feel trapped in an unwanted living arrangement, in which their adult children take advantage of their hospitality without offering much in exchange.

The parents' location has a significant impact on the likelihood that at least one of their adult children will live with them. Specifically, parents who reside in the largest census metropolitan areas (CMAs) are more likely to have an adult child at home. In Canada, that translates to: 41% of parents in Vancouver; 39% in Toronto; 34% in Ottawa; and 28% in Montréal. In contrast, only 17% of parents living in rural areas or small towns share their house with at least one of their adult children.

These results do not necessarily mean that parents who reside in smaller places are more reluctant to accommodate their adult children. Most post-secondary institutions are located in larger cities and for college or university students whose parents already live in a CMA, staying at home can be a financially attractive option. For some students, it might even be the only option. Young adults from more remote regions don't usually have that choice and many have to leave home to pursue higher education. But that doesn't mean adult children won't be moving back home after school.

The province or state of residence also affects the likelihood of parents having an adult child or children living at home. In Ontario, parents had a 30% chance having an adult child at home; in contrast, the probability was significantly lower in the Canadian Prairies (17%).

With all this in mind, the chances of adult children being financially stable when their parents retire are decreasing. It's becoming increasingly important for parents to plan for an independent retirement.

The Excuse Maker:

Many people blame circumstances for their inability to set money aside for retirement. But the truth is, no matter what you earn, you can always contribute at least a little bit. Regular contributions to a retirement plan are ultimately your responsibility. This is the case whether or not you feel the government fails to provide for your well-being, your boss doesn't pay you enough, you were born unlucky, your parents were unable to provide adequate financial support, or your dire financial situation is caused by society. Only you can take care of yourself in the future.

My Rule of Thumb

Why are you financially challenged?

Rumour has it that Joseph Kennedy Sr. – a prominent businessman and political figure, and the father of U.S. President John F. Kennedy – made his millions from the sale of his stock holdings before the great market crash of the great depression

One day he was having his shoes polished. The shoe polisher was boasting about how easy it was to make money in the stock market. After the encounter, Kennedy decided to sell all of his stock holdings; the market crashed shortly after. What was his reason for selling? He reasoned that if a shoe maker who obviously had no knowledge of stock market is professing his investment expertise, then every Tom, Dick and Harry is probably feeling just as savvy. He concluded that the market must be too hot and too high, so it was time to sell.

After the market crashed, with the cash he garnered from the stocks he sold, he bought a lot of quality stocks at rock-bottom prices; these later accounted for his great fortune.

This story befits the rule of thumb.

Most of us tend to take financial advice from peers, neighbours, co-workers, and family members. But most of these sources (95%) are actually financially challenged. Your friends and loved ones might mean well, but generally they are financially uneducated. If they have not achieved financial success themselves, then you can't subject your financial security to their advice.

Irrationality seems to be part of our instinct. When we are sick, we seek medical advice from a physician rather than a hospital orderly, but when it comes to financial matters, our immediate instinct is to talk to those who are equally financially challenged, and often worse off financially than ourselves. We lose our rationale and let emotion dictate our course of action.

The advice we give to our clients is to follow this rule of thumb: Only seek advice from the top 5% of financially secure people and/or from a qualified Financial Planner or Advisor.

How Money Works

Now that you might have identified a weakness in your approach to finances, let's see how money works. Most people are concerned about money matters, but few truly understand how money works.

When it comes to finances, how much do you know?

If you're like most people, you probably know very little about personal finance. Perhaps you think long-term security is impossible on your income. But, the truth is, no matter what your income level is you can achieve financial security. You just have to take the time to learn a few simple principles about how money works.

Financial education is for everyone

I believe that there should be no "secrets" to financial security. Financial education isn't just for the wealthy. My goal is to educate hardworking families — just like yours — about simple concepts that can change your financial future forever.

Do you know when you need life insurance the most? Have you started planning for retirement? Do you know how much something really costs when you put it on your credit card? Taking a few moments to learn some simple concepts about how money works can save you from financial headaches later. Learn more about how money works with the financial concepts below. They're simple!

Buy Term and Invest the Difference

The "Buy Term and Invest the Difference" philosophy encourages families to purchase affordable term life insurance. This way they can then have more money to invest in the family's future.

Instead of buying into cash value policies that bundle investments with life insurance, you should keep investments and life insurance separate. This way, families can have a clear picture of how secure their financial future is.

Whole life or Universal life products may provide alternative investment vehicles for those who have already maximized their RRSP (or 401k) and TFSA contributions; these products also offer useful tools to cover tax liabilities arising from the estate of wealthy folks, i.e. the top 5% of the population.

Theory of Decreasing Responsibilities

According to the "Theory of Decreasing Responsibilities," your need for life insurance peaks along with your family responsibilities.

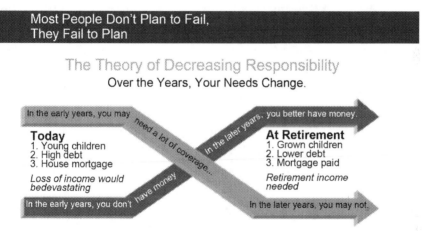

When you're young, you may have children to support, a new mortgage to manage, and many other obligations. All this when you haven't had the time to accumulate much money! This is the time when the death of a breadwinner or caretaker could be most devastating and when you need insurance coverage the most.

When you're older, you usually have fewer dependents and fewer financial responsibilities. Plus, you've had years to accumulate wealth through savings and investments. At this point, your need for insurance has reduced dramatically, and you have your own funds to see you through your retirement years. So make sure you only get enough coverage to meet your needs.

The Cost of Convenience

How much do you pay for convenience? When you put a purchase on your credit card, you may think it's the most convenient way to pay. But think again. The interest that you could end up owing on that credit card could make your purchase cost a lot more than you originally thought!

You need to realise that you end up paying a lot of hard-earned money just for the convenience of saying, "Charge it." That's why it's so important to build up savings for purchases in order to avoid "The Cost of Convenience".

The Rule of 72

Do you know the "Rule of 72" and how it works? The "Rule of 72" is an easy way to approximate how long it will take your savings to double. Just divide 72 by the interest rate you earn to determine the number of years it will take for your money to double. It shows you how much faster money can grow with a higher rate of return.

By using the Rule of 72, you can see why it pays to fight for every extra percentage point of interest you can get. Once you know your rate, use the "Rule of 72" to compute how fast YOUR savings will double!

The Rule of 72

Approximates the number of years it takes to double your money.

72 ÷ 3%	72 ÷ 6%	72 ÷ 12%
24 years	**12 years**	**6 years**

0 yr $10,000	0 yr $10,000	0 yr $10,000
		6 yr $20,000
	12 yr $20,000	12 yr $40,000
		18 yr $80,000
24yr $20,000	24 yr $40,000	24 yr $160,000
		30 yr $320,000
	36 yr $80,000	36 yr $640,000
		42 yr $1,280,000
48 yr $40,000	48 yr $160,000	48 yr $2,560,000

Strategic Investment Planning

Strategic investment planning can take the worry out of market fluctuations. Long-term investors will experience every phase of a market cycle. They should anticipate the up and down swings, as these are part of normal market activity. Fortunately, long-term investments are able to ride out the ups and downs. Strategic investment planning takes the worry out of market fluctuations, and regular contributions allow you to get the most out of your investments. This is because, historically, markets have gone up. Over 30 years from 1977 to 2007, the S&P/ TSX Composite Total Return Index 12.6% per year. So when markets drop, savvy investors recognize the opportunity to increase their holdings at lower prices and when the market rises again, those who held on to their investments reap the rewards. The best way to approach your investment plan is to craft a sound portfolio that suits your risk tolerance so you can handle the market's inevitable fluctuations.

The following eight strategies will help you feel more comfortable when the markets are turbulent.

1. Focus on the long term --- Your best approach is to stick with your long-term investment plan and remain focused on your goals. While daily market swings may cause some concern, if you are confident that your plan is tailored to your risk tolerance, when the market fluctuates the returns generated will generally remain within your comfort level. A long-term strategic investment plan states your goals and defines your terms: how much and how often you will invest, and what type of investments you want to contribute to. This plan encompasses not only investments, but also taxation and estate planning. It is meant to help you feel secure about your finances and your future.

2. Invest regularly --- One of the most important components of investing successfully is following a regular schedule. Even small amounts invested regularly accumulate to large sums over time.

3. Take advantage of dollar cost averaging --- This is a timing strategy of investing equal dollar amounts regularly (such as $100 monthly) over lengthy time periods in a particular investment or portfolio. By doing so, more shares are purchased when prices are low and fewer shares are purchased when prices are high. The point of this is to lower the total average *cost per share* of the investment, giving the investor a lower overall cost for the shares purchased over time.

4. An optimal asset mix — Your optimal asset mix refers to the combination of equity and fixed income investments you want to invest in, given your particular risk tolerance. Different assets have varying degrees of volatility and tend to react differently to market conditions. By holding a mix of assets, you can maintain a volatility level that you're comfortable with, and still be in a position to benefit from whatever asset class the market favours at any given time.

5. Diversify at home and abroad — Optimal asset allocation includes diversification. Mutual funds are great because they provide a ready-made, diverse investment. Holding more than one type of fund within each asset class can increase diversification. Our Strategic Investment Planning approach enables you to diversify in order to produce an optimal portfolio, regardless of how risk tolerant or risk-averse you might be. To capitalize on some of the international investment opportunities available, and further increase the diversification of your portfolio, hold mutual funds that invest outside of your country as well as at home.

6. Set goals for motivation — A unique optimal asset mix should be crafted for each of your financial goals. Perhaps you want to accumulate funds for your retirement or save for a child's education. Maybe you want to finance your own business. Such quantifiable goals can be a great motivation when markets are turbulent. Having invested regularly and seen your savings increase, you can see what progress you've made since you started investing and reassure yourself that you're well on your way to reaching your goals.

7. Work with a trusted Financial Planner — Always work with a Certified Financial Planner when devising an investment plan to meet your long term goals. Unfortunately, the majority of financial advisors or consultants are not Certified Financial Planners. Many of these financial advisors are licensed only as sales people, and work to sell investment products. Alternatively, Certified Financial Planners must undergo very challenging professional examinations and have acquired years of financial planning experience. Don't put your money into the hands of an advisor with a hidden agenda.

8. *Financial Health Check* — Once your investment plan is up and running, be sure to review your progress at least once a year. An annual check-up is a good time for us to revisit your goals and investment time horizon and reassess your risk tolerance. Doing so allows us to assess your investments and fine-tune your plan, rebalancing your portfolio if necessary. It is a good idea to rebalance your portfolio periodically in order to ensure the asset mix you originally invested in still reflects your tolerance for risk.

The bottom line:

It's much easier — and much more rewarding — to stay invested. When you understand that both highs and lows offer rewards, you'll see that it's always a good time to be in the market. Patience is the key to success through all stages of the market cycle, and your perseverance will allow you to benefit from the market's upswings when they occur. Staying with your long-term strategic investment plan will keep you on the road to achieving your financial goals.

Mastering the Bank and the Tax Agency:
How to Manage your Relationship with the Two Greatest Deterrents to Your Wealth Accumulation Goal

A dying man summoned his Lawyer and Accountant to his bedside. He turned to his Lawyer and said, "I'd like to change something in my will before I go." The lawyer responded, "Of course, anything you wish. What change needs to be made?" To this the dying man replied, "Instead of having a burial, I want to be cremated." The man's lawyer asked him what he would like done with the ashes. The dying man answered, "I want you to deliver my ashes to my Banker and the CRA/IRS; they have taken everything from me, I might as well give them my ashes – they're the last tangible things I've got!"

This joke may seem ridiculous, but Tax and Financial Costs can take up to 70% of your family's gross income. On average, each and every North American is working for the taxman and the banker directly and indirectly up to 70% of their working life time. Put another way, each one of us is paying 70% of our whole life income to the taxman and the banker. Unless (and until) you learn how to manage these expenses, you may be living pay cheque to pay cheque. The only solution is to seek advice from Tax and Financial Professionals.

Income distribution

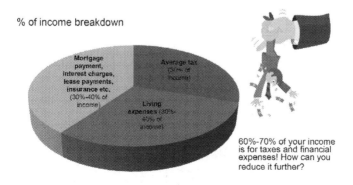

% of income breakdown

Mortgage payment, interest charges, lease payments, insurance etc. (30%-40% of income)

Average tax (30% of income)

Living expenses (30%-40% of income)

60%-70% of your income is for taxes and financial expenses! How can you reduce it further?

Let's consider your current relationship with the bank and the tax agency.

The Bank:

In addition to an average tax rate of 30% from your income, a big chunk of your after tax income (35% to 40%) is spent on financial costs, such as: mortgage, credit cards, insurance, interest charges, and bank charges and fees; most of which are incurred at the bank.

Until you know how to manage tax and financial costs efficiently, you may be in a perpetual cycle of living pay cheque to pay cheque.

When you consider that most credit cards charge 15% to 20% in interest, and that banks only pay us 2-3% per annum from a GIC (Guaranteed Investment Certificate), it's easy to think it's impossible to win "the money game" against banks and the tax agency. GICs are often promoted by banks for their low risk and guaranteed returns, but with returns that hardly match the inflation rate, a more appropriate phrase for the GIC acronym might be "Guaranteed Insufficient Cash." Canadians have invested more than one trillion dollars in GICs at banks –and Americans have been just as easily swindled. That might explain why banks make billions in profits every year while many of their customers are struggling financially. Storing your money in a GIC means the opportunity cost on alternative investments is lost.

Another way your bank misleads you is by providing a mortgage for your home, rather than a secured line of credit; the resulting interest charges paid over the amortized period make up at least 1.5 times the cost of your home. If offered lines of credit at the same interest rates as home loans, we could save thousands to hundreds of thousands in interest charges and reduce the repayment period by half. This link to a short Smart Equity video breaks down how this is possible: http://www.inlinebusiness.com/cgi-bin/d.cgi/comcorp/demo2.html or http://www.smartequitysales.com

Banks provide both lines of credit and mortgages. Even though the Line of Credit (LOC) is the better option for clients, the Mortgage is the product banks recommend. This is because when their clients sign up for mortgages, banks profit because they have locked clients into high interest charges for the next 25-35 years. You know, as a client, that it would be much more beneficial to be a shareholder of a bank, which would entitle you to a share of the bank's riches, than to lend money to banks to make incredible profits at your expense. But banks are so powerful that it can seem impossible to demand more.

As consumers, we are placed in an uneven playing field with banks in the money game. Even if we are abused by banks, we cannot win because we cannot afford to take the bank to court. The bank, having more money, would ultimately win any court battle because they could hire top legal advisors.

We are also kept in the dark. Most North Americans put a large portion of their investments in the care of banks out of ignorance. But clients do not receive personalized investment and financial planning advice from the banks they invest in. Banks aim to provide counter service, and do not adopt a personalized approach unless you have $250,000 or more in their possession. They might promise personalized financial planning services if you threaten to pull out your investments, but this is just a strategy to keep your accounts. Except in exceptional cases, the bank's financial advisors assigned to your accounts don't do a periodic financial and investment plan review with you. And as the investor, you deserve to be consulted.

Ultimately you pay banks, directly or indirectly, to provide you with financial and investment planning services. Ask yourself what you get in return for these payments. Even though qualified Financial Planners cum Tax Accountants are what clients need, banks do not have qualified advisors who are competent in taxation and financial planning at the branch to provide the expertise you need; the pay structure and/or organizational structure at the branches are not conducive to recruit such talents.

Have you asked your bank to justify your fee payments? So often, we put so much trust in banks that we never ask for our basic right as an investor or consumer. Because these low-level services have become standard, we have been lead to believe that this is the service we deserve for paying 35% to 40% of our after-tax income to banks.

If your doctor, dentist, accountant, lawyer, or supplier provided the same level of service, you would demand better service, take your business elsewhere, or even contemplate legal action. These costs are small in comparison to those financial costs incurred at banks, but we accept whatever level of service is deemed sufficient by the banks.

The Tax Agency:

Many of us do not understand the value in hiring qualified tax professionals. We often neglect the fact that tax filing is only the last step in a complex tax deferral and minimization planning process. Without a qualified tax accountant, you may not optimize your tax deferral and minimization strategies. Essentially, you may be losing money.

Taxation is not as simple as it seems. Tax professionals spend years of training, receiving certification and enrolling in continuous professional development courses to keep abreast of changes to the Income Tax Act and budgets. Using qualified tax professionals greatly decreases your chance of being audited by the tax agency and helps you avoid subsequent tax return amendments, which are often a result of errors and omissions made by self-filing products or tax preparers.

Taxes account for a large percentage of your expenditure. The average tax payer loses 30% of his income to taxes. Surely such a sizable amount deserves scrutiny and careful planning. Given that there can be so much to gain by referring to a professional, do you feel competent enough to take advantage of all tax credits, deferral and minimization techniques? There's no sense in giving the government more money than necessary.

Without incorporating a qualified tax professional in your tax minimization strategy, you may be tax inefficient, making it difficult,

31

and sometimes impossible, to free up any surplus money for investments to achieve your financial goals.

The fee charged to engage with a tax professional is well justified in terms of tax savings, but it's important to find someone qualified for your needs. When you have a heart problem, you seek the expertise of a heart doctor, not a foot doctor, so apply the same approach to your finances. To get the best for your money, choose a Certified Accountant from one of the three recognized accounting bodies (CA, CGA & CMA) to help you take advantage of tax deferral and tax minimization strategies. Tax preparers are not regulated, nor do they require stringent training or certification. Anyone can claim his or her expertise as a tax preparer without having gone through proper professional training or certification. Protect your money. Don't lose to the tax agency, and choose an advisor you can trust.

Conclusion:

Even though you have contributed to their profits and bonuses your whole life, the bank will not give you money when you are broke during retirement. And don't expect the Government to honour you for being tax foolish. Your finances are in your hands.

Many people are "Penny wise, pound foolish." They know how to save their pennies, but don't think about their finances as a whole. They think they can't afford to hire a tax professional or financial planner, but don't consider how much of their money they lose to the Tax Agency and the Bank.

Tax and financial costs constitute 65% to 70% of your income. I can safely predict that unless you can manage these relationships effectively, you will never achieve your financial goals, no matter how much you earn.

Why Paying Down your Mortgage is Not a Sound Decision

The question of whether you should pay down a mortgage or contribute to an RRSP, 401k, TFSA, or non-registered investment generates a lot of debate.

Finally we have an answer. Most experts have voted in favour of investments, based on two simple economic concepts:

1.   Money is used most tax efficiently

When you contribute to your RRSP, 401k, or pension plan, you get an instant rate of return. This is a benefit available even for those in the top marginal tax bracket. Contributing to retirement is the better choice even if the return on your investment is lower than the interest rate of your mortgage. When you factor in the re-investment rate of return of your tax refund, paying down your mortgage is a poor option.

2.   Opportunity cost

Over the past 50 years, the historical average mortgage interest rate has been lower than the returns from the S&P/TSX Composite Total Return Index. This means, if the future follows a similar pattern, investments could potentially earn a higher rate of return.

I have always reminded my clients:

1.   A mortgage-free home does not pay for food or cover living expenses during retirement. If you don't have enough retirement savings to get by, you can't bring a brick or kitchen tile to your local grocer in exchange for food.
2.   If you're thinking that downsizing and using equity from your home to support yourself after you retire is a good plan to cover living expenses, you are in for a rude awakening. A $200,000 value in home equity might last 5-6 years at the most.

3.   By contributing to investment options while you pay down your mortgage, you get the best deal. By the time you retire your home should be fully paid for (or you'll only have a few payments left) and you'll enjoy the security of sizeable retirement savings. This simply isn't a possibility for those who pay off their mortgages before thinking about retirement.

4.   Your best move would be to shift your focus to retirement as long as mortgage rates are lower than investment returns.

Why Real Estate is Not a Good Investment:

Sound Advice for Potential and Existing Homeowners

PERCEPTION

"Real estate provides better returns than equities."

REALITY: POOR PRICE PERFORMANCE

Over the last 40 years, Canadian residential real estate has only produced an average annual return of 0.2% after inflation. In comparison, the Canadian stock market has gained a very respectable 4.4% after inflation.

REAL ESTATE	S&P/TSX TR	DIFFERENCE
(After Inflation)	(After Inflation)	In Returns
0.2%	4.4%	4.2%

* S&P/TSX Total Return Index.

PERCEPTION

"Real estate is a 'can't miss' investment that produces steady gains over time."

REALITY: DECLINING RETURNS

Returns on rental housing investments in Canada have declined over time.

2001	2002	2003
12.4%	9.9%	5.1%

PERCEPTION

"Interest rates are so low, so I can afford to take on

REALITY: INTEREST RATES RISK INCREASES

Except for the past 3 years, when the interest rate was deliberately kept artificially low to stimulate the economy,

a bigger mortgage."   five-year mortgage rates in Canada from
                         1954 to 2004 ranged from 6% to 19%
                         (1983)

A large percentage of Canadians' net wealth is in real estate – the same is true of Americans. In Canada that is 28%, compared to 62% in financial assets[1]. But, as demonstrated by the chart above, there's **perception** and then there's **reality**. Making sound financial choices is all about closing the gap between the two. Too often people's actions are informed by common misconceptions. As a potential new homeowner or an existing homeowner looking to trade up, if you want to act according to reality, it's a good idea to evaluate any real estate decision through the lenses of **perspective**, **prudence**, and **balance**.

1) Gain Perspective – Price Performance

As noted above, over the last 40 years Canadian residential real estate has only produced an average annual return of 0.2% after inflation. This compares to the Canadian stock market which earned, on average, 4.4% after inflation. Surely this is sufficient evidence to prove that potential gains can be more fruitful if your money is invested in the stock market rather than real estate.

2) Emphasize Prudence – Minimize Your Risks

Since price performance can vary widely from decade to decade, depending on the rise or fall in housing demand, deciding when you enter the real estate market can elevate or diminish your risks. Consider these factors when deciding whether it's a good idea to purchase a residential property in the near future.

Weakening demand for housing:

---

[1] This article used statistics from the following sources:
1. AGF Funds Inc., Bank of Canada, 2004 Clayton Research based on data from Statistics Canada CMCH.
2. 2004 Clayton Research based on data from Statistics Canada.

- Pent-up housing demand from first-time homeowners has mostly been absorbed. This reinforces the belief that we've passed an important peak in short-term demand.
- Over the next five to ten years it's forecasted that there will be weakened housing demand related to the slowing of the overall population growth. This effect will be somewhat offset by continuing immigration, but this applies mostly to larger urban centers.

Beware of interest rates:

Today we have historically low mortgage rates, but when today's mortgages come up for renewal several years from now, interest rates will more than likely be higher. This can greatly impact your monthly mortgage payments, especially if you have a high-ratio mortgage (less than 25% down).

As shown below, a 1% rise in your interest rate can increase your monthly mortgage payment by as much as 12.23%.

$200,000 mortgage; 5 year term; 30 year amortization	4%	5%	% increase
Monthly payment	$951.04	$1,067.39	12.23%

3) Stress Balance – Real Estate and Your Other Assets

Think of real estate as an asset. In order for you to get a better picture of your asset balance, ensure that your real estate holdings are included in your overall asset allocation plan.

- **Follow the 30% rule:** As a general rule, if you subtract your mortgage from the value of your real estate the number should account for no more than 30% of your total assets.

- **Asset diversification:** Real estate offers an additional level of diversification in any portfolio, but you must be careful not to overdo it.

- Any prudent decision involving real estate needs to be tailored to you. Below are some simple exercises to help guide you in making sound choices about real estate decisions.

- **Ensure your assets are balanced.** Because so much money is required to purchase a house, real estate is necessarily part of your overall wealth. It should be balanced against other asset classes – stocks, bonds, and cash – to ensure steady, even gains in your portfolio. In Canada the average household had approximately 28% of its net worth in real estate in 2003. This is a good guideline to follow.

- **Calculate the Appropriate Ratios.** The ability to consistently cover your mortgage payments with a reasonable safety margin is paramount. Ensure that your mortgage payments are easy to meet and that your income can service your debt. Most lenders prefer a homebuyer who does not exceed a certain threshold of debt, so make sure you are living well within your means in order to be a desirable candidate, and to be able to manage expenses in case of a decrease in income.

YOUR HOUSEHOLD INCOME	YOUR TOTAL DEBT PAYMENTS
	EXISTING DEBT PAYMENTS/EXPENSES
	HEATING COSTS
	PROPOSED PRIMARY RESIDENCE MORTGAGE PAYMENTS

The Total Debt Service Ratio is the measure of total household debt expenses (existing debt expenses, mortgage payments, heating costs, etc.) to total income. These expenses should account for no more than **37%** of your total income.

Some sound advice I can offer you is this: Think of real estate primarily as a way to meet lifestyle needs, not investment goals. If you think about it this way, you should be able to put to use the skills of **perspective**, **prudence**, and **balance**.

The Potential Canadian Housing Bubble of 2010/2011

A housing bubble refers to the rapid, artificial increase in property values that eventually reach levels that are unsustainable on homeowners' incomes. Like a bubble, prices grow and grow until the inevitable burst. Canada is currently enabling the growth of such a bubble through some of its real estate practices. Here are some issues that are cause for concern.

For one thing, credit is easily obtained, and easy credit leads to overpricing. When anyone can buy a home, prices rise because houses are in demand. Home ownership in Canada recently reached 64%. This is the highest in the world! Now, this would perhaps be great news if not for the fact that 30% of Canadian households do not pay income taxes because their earnings are under the low income threshold. In other words, practically 90% of those above the low income threshold own a home. Forgive me for saying so, but we seem to be heading toward the so-called Utopia of socialist ideals which failed in former communist regimes, such as in USSR, Communist China, Vietnam, and Cuba.

In our society this could be a recipe for disaster. If people are unable to make their mortgage payments, foreclosures will proliferate. Foreclosures bring down the value of neighbours' houses and also leave previous homeowners in an undesirable financial position. They will be plagued by poor credit scores and will find it difficult to get ahead in the future. Banks need to be more selective when considering candidates for loans. When criteria are too lenient, everyone suffers. What good does it do to let people at risk of financial troubles get in over their heads?

But the banks don't suffer, so nothing is done. The Canadian government is driving this bubble. CMHC (the Canada Mortgage and Housing Corporation) provides insurance to banks. CMHC has been buying so many products; one of these products is Ottawa's Insured Mortgage Program, which has bought more than $65 billion from the banks. This is a huge liquidity dump from the Government into the housing market.

So, since the banks aren't taking on risks by offering loans to high-risk homebuyers, people are encouraged to take on debt they can't afford. In fact, rock-bottom interest rates were deliberately set by the Government to boost economy recovery. And of course people took the opportunity to purchase homes, even though they weren't prepared to handle the responsibilities of home-ownership. Now, impending HST in Ontario and BC is adding fuel to an already hot market.

Low threshold, 5% down payments and amortization periods of up to 35 years (previously 40 years) practically qualify every Tom, Dick, and Harry to buy a home or rental property. In fact, the majority of first time buyers (90%) used a 35 year amortization period and two-thirds (66.7%) had down payments of only 5%. Yet, no policy maker dares to acknowledge that misguided government policy typically aids and abets bubble formation. Imagine the political backlash that would occur if a politician or central banker told homeowners their houses are worth 20% less than they thought they were. With so little equity in their homes, homeowners would owe much more than they bargained for.

Unfortunately, when it comes to home ownership, most people are caught on an emotional roller coaster that keeps them from making informed decisions about buying and selling homes. This is part of the reason so many people end up in houses worth less than what they're paying. People often end up working contrary to the "buy low, sell high" concept everyone preaches, and tend to buy on upturns and sell on downturns for these reasons:

- They believe that they could "miss the boat" if they don't act right away during an upturn. Alternatively, they might sell to avoid a bottomless pit during the downturn. Either way they become victims of their emotions. Rather than being patient, they submit to worry.

- They succumbed to family and peer pressure to become homeowners without properly evaluating the carrying costs of home ownership. Such costs include: property tax, condo fees, utilities, insurance, repairs, maintenance, etc.

- They tend to seek advice from people who are equally naive or they put their money into the hands of someone who is essentially a licensed sales representative, trained only to sell real estate. They are also unaware of some of the practices of the existing real estate brokerage system. The transaction oriented representative or broker depends on transactions to generate commission income.

When you consider all of the issues mentioned above, it becomes clear that Canada might be heading toward its own housing crisis in the near future. Without exercising restraint, we only increase personal debt and make financial stability more difficult for Canadians. The Canadian government has stepped in – in order to slow the increasing debt load of Canadians who purchase houses thanks to low interest, rather than affordability or the ability to meet mortgage payments when the interest rates rise, the Canadian Federal Government has increase the minimum down payment from 5% to 10%, effective April 1, 2010. However, only homeowners can determine what is reasonable for them. The bubble is growing and if we don't exercise control, it's sure to burst soon.

How to Avoid a Tax Audit

How can you send in the best personal tax return?

1. File On Time: Don't file too early or too late

If you file too early, your file is more likely to catch the attention of CRA or IRS tax employees, who are bunkered down during the cold winter months since it is neither the vacation season nor their busy season.

File too late and you'll have to pay interest on any tax owed. You'll also increase your odds of being audited.

2. Keep Track of Receipts

CRA and IRS employees will usually notice any deviations from your usual year to year filings, so make sure you have documentation to account for them.

3. Stay On Top of New Deductions and Credits

Various new credits have been introduced over the past few years, such as credits for transit passes and home renovations. Individuals should think about filing as a family unit to take advantage of all available deductions and credits.

Students can transfer tuition, education, and book amounts to a supporting spouse, parent, or grandparent.

Medical Expenses for one individual can be transferred to a supporting earner.

4. Be Aware Of Investment and Donation Schemes

Take advantage of deductions and credits but always avoid anything too incredible. Things that seem too good to be true usually are.

There are a lot of investment and tax schemes that are taking place. For example, some might boast: "Give $5,000 and you'll get a donation receipt for $30,000." Such claims are red flags on tax returns. Most people who take part are audited and end up having to pay back their refunds along with interest and penalties.

Job Loss

Whether you were expecting it or not; whether your first reaction was shock or anger, the best thing you can do for yourself is come to terms with your loss and get past it as soon as you can. One way of moving on is to consider the blessing your job loss might actually be. Many people become self-employed or change careers after termination. Now that you have the opportunity to start over again, ask yourself what you might do differently.

Of course job loss forces us to consider some questions we might not have contemplated before. For example: How can you handle your severance package in the most tax efficient way? How will you manage cash flow so that you have enough to live on, without exhausting your resources? Which benefits should you replace privately?

If you plan on returning to the work place right away, you also have to consider the fact that you have just experienced a very difficult change in your life. So often our occupations help to form our identities. Your sense of security, as well as your sense of self-worth, might have taken a hit. It can be tempting to start sending out resumes and registering with employment consultants right away, but you might need to take some time to regain your confidence before you go to your first interview. If you haven't competed for a work position in awhile, you might want to upgrade your skills.

Severance

If you were "downsized," you probably received some severance pay. As with any large sum you receive, it's important to plan to spend it wisely. Remember that your severance pay can have a major impact on either the quality of your retirement or your standard of living while you search for a new opportunity. Be sure to talk to a tax accountant as soon as possible in order to minimize your tax liabilities and maximize the money that is available to you.

Though you might be able to count on some severance pay, you might not be able to predict the exact amount. The most important factor to remember is that the total amount is usually fully taxable in the year you receive your severance. There may be ways to defer tax on some or all of your severance pay, so consult your financial advisor for details.

Pension Benefits

You might be entitled to some or all of the pension benefits you accumulated at the company you worked for. Up to 75% of employees today do not have an employer- sponsored pension benefit plan, but for those who did enjoy such benefits, you have some options. You might be able to collect a reduced pension now or a full pension later. Additionally you might be able to transfer the full value (both your own and your employer's contributions made on your behalf) to another retirement plan, such as a Locked in Retirement Account, or the pension plan of a new employer, if available.

If your benefits haven't vested, you will be entitled to a refund of the amount you contributed yourself. You can elect to take a taxable cash settlement or to transfer your benefits on a tax-deferred basis to another retirement plan. If you don't need the cash now, you could end up paying more tax than necessary. You'll want to choose the option that most effectively defers taxes. With proper taxation advice, you can make sure you keep more for yourself and give less to the taxman.

A New Budget

Without regular employment income, you could find yourself living on a lot less. Funds might be limited for a long time, and you might have to stick to a strict budget for longer than you had anticipated. Getting by on less isn't easy, but a financial planner might be able to assess your situation and provide financial solutions to the challenges you are facing. There are a few things you will have to think about:

- **Debt management** – If you are carrying debt at a high interest rate, consider consolidating all of your debts under a single umbrella loan. Doing so can lower your interest rate, so that you will end up paying less interest over time.
- **Restructuring** – In some cases, it is possible to restructure your debts to make the interest on the loan tax deductible.
- **Retirement Withdrawals** – Any money you take out of your Registered Retirement Savings Plan becomes fully taxable, so it's best to avoid making withdrawals unless you absolutely need to. Consider withdrawing from a Tax-Free Savings Account (TFSA) on a tax-free basis. This way you can re-pay the borrowed amount in the future year if you choose.

Investing

The lump sum you receive as severance could have major tax and financial implications, depending on your decision:

- **Retiring early** – If you opt for early retirement, your goal will likely be to invest for the long-term, with a view to augmenting your retirement income. Plan accordingly, and seek the help of a financial advisor.
- **Searching for a job** – You might need your severance package to manage your household bills until you find new employment. A short-term, easily accessible investment might be your best option if this is the case.
- **Taking a job** – If you find a new job quickly, it's a good idea to invest your entire severance package.
- **Becoming your own boss** – If you plan on starting your own business, you might need to use some (or all) of your severance package to finance it. Try to keep some of your severance investments relatively liquid and secure, so you'll have something to fall back on in case your venture doesn't work out as you hope.

Early Retirement

If you're in your early 60s or late 50s and you feel like you have been forced into retirement, you must take stock of your situation immediately. Your retirement savings will have to last longer, and you will be retiring with fewer resources than you'd originally planned. Retirement can allow you time to do some of the things you've dreamed of, but you'll have to determine whether or not you'll have the resources to make those dreams come true. These are some of the questions you'll need to consider:

- How can I make sure I have enough money to see me through retirement?
- How can I protect myself and my family against the effects of inflation over a retirement that could last as long as 40 years?
- Should I downsize my home and invest the free-up equity to increase my retirement assets?
- Does part-time work, or starting my own business, make more sense for me?
- Should I convert my RRSP (or 401k) or TFSA into retirement income now or later?

Self-Employment

Running a successful business requires many attributes of the business owner: discipline, focus, perseverance, entrepreneurial ability, and hard work. You'll probably have to take on much more risk, work longer hours, make many sacrifices, and use a significant amount of start-up capital. Be sure that you can be comfortable with the entrepreneurial lifestyle!

Make a Plan

When you have moved past your job loss remember that no matter how secure you might feel in your new position, life is unpredictable. Preparing for the unknown can help you feel secure and can make managing troubling times more comfortable. While you're employed, set up a short-term investment fund that will last for three to nine months of unemployment. It's important to stay on top of your overall financial plan, and to keep it updated with recent changes in your circumstances. Stay positive and do not lose sight of the bigger picture.

SEVERANCE TAX-SAVING TIPS

Talk to your financial advisor about the ways you can protect your severance package against taxes. Consider the following possibilities:

- **Transfer as much of your severance as possible into your retirement account:** A financial planner can determine if you qualify for the retiring allowance rollover.
- **Split income with your spouse:** If one of you is now earning a higher income than the other, consider a spousal RRSP
- **Contribute to your retirement account:** If you have contribution room available or a pension adjustment reversal as a result of the termination of your participation in a pension plan, consider investing some or all of your severance payment in an RRSP.
- **Contribute to a TFSA:** The Tax-Free Savings Account allows you to save for retirement and emergencies such as job loss.

Your Future

You might find this section a little repetitive, but it's only because I want readers to understand how important it is to plan for your later life! Personal financial planning provides you with a method for organising your financial future, so you can plan for the unforeseen. Organizing your finances empowers you to be independent and handle unpredicted events in your life. Successful personal financial planning is crucial for anyone who wishes to manage financial difficulties and accumulate wealth.

Without doubt personal finance is a daunting subject and is difficult to comprehend fully, so it is no wonder that so many are inclined to shy away from taking responsibility for their financial lives. But if you never take the time to learn about how your money can work for you, you will never be able to take advantage of its capacity. As with everything in life, a little effort goes a long way. Resolving to rid yourself of financial stress is a courageous choice; it takes discipline and dedication to achieve financial freedom. But once you realise that having a well-developed financial plan is central to a prosperous financial future, it becomes easier to commit to saving.

Financial planning is an integrated, personal approach to an individual's well-being. Turning vague goals into concrete plans is like highlighting a route for a road trip on a map. It lets you see how you can reach your destination, while allowing for some interesting pit stops along the way. Creating attainable, measurable goals is the first thing you'll need to do in order to achieve financial security. One task of financial planning is to help you identify the important numbers: How much do you need to save, and by when? Not knowing what you have to do to achieve your goals, how much you'll need to save in order to live comfortably when you retire for example, can trigger anxiety. When you have a clear idea of how much you need to put away each month you can make changes in your budget in order to follow your plan and enjoy the peace of mind that accompanies fiscal mastery.

In order to prepare your financial plan for the future, you'll need to discover where you are today. Pull out all of your accounts and determine how much money you have saved up, the value of your investments, and what types of investment vehicles hold your money. This will give you a blueprint that will help you make plans to achieve your goals. By assessing how effective your investments are and comparing different investment vehicles, you will be able to clarify what products you should be investing in and determine the risk levels you're willing to commit to, depending on when you'll need to access your savings. A financial blueprint will provide you with a clear picture so that you can figure out how to better manage your finances beginning today.

The future is always uncertain, but in today's global climate, which spells uncertainty wherever you turn, that fact makes financial security increasingly important. Just look at the credit crunch crisis. Because people were not prepared for a turbulent future, many have suffered the consequences. Keep this in mind when you are planning your finances, especially when making arrangements for your retirement savings. Security and financial comfort can be achieved through a good plan that will withstand the toughest of times.

Financial planning can enrich your life. Three reasons why:

- Most of us are reluctant to talk about retirement. Wanting to avoid the subject is understandable – we try not to think about problems that might occur after we retire because we know we won't have a steady income from employment to get us back on track – but the reality is at some point we will have to realise that in addition to leisure retirement brings its own set of problems, and possibly disasters. Recognizing potential difficulties now can help you make changes before you encounter problems. Planning for your retirement isn't just about crunching numbers; you're planning for your golden years! To make those years the most enriching, look at your lifestyle now and tweak your current finances and investments to secure a comfortable future. If you choose to work after retirement it should be done willingly to learn something new or stay active within your community. You don't want to end up working because your finances aren't in check.

- Planning for retirement isn't just about planning for the years after you've finished working; it also gives you a sense of comfort and security in the years leading to your retirement. Planning for retirement reassures you of a financially stable future in which you will have the freedom to pursue the things you always wanted to without worrying about making the smartest career moves. It also relieves your family and loved ones of the pressure to take care of you as you age. This is a benefit to you as well as your loved ones. After a life of independence it can be humbling to put yourself in the care of others. Life after retirement should be just as fulfilling as life before this milestone.

- Financial planning, especially when tackled at an early age, can help give your life focus and help you achieve your short and long-term goals. Financial planning gives you a set of tools to create wealth and build a nest egg that you can use in case of an emergency. Being an active participant in your financial planning also gives you the ability to make informed decisions about investments. When you take control of your financial future you can avoid mistakes and reap the benefits for the rest of your life.

Financial planning and retirement planning work hand in hand. Both must be given serious consideration and put into action in order to live a comfortable life. Securing your future and making your money work for you are two valuable commodities, and two powerful reasons why financial planning and retirement planning is important.

A Few Words of Caution:

When planning for your financial present and future, it's important to seek a qualified professional, such as a Certified Financial

Planner. Your financial security is at stake and you don't want to fall into the trap of putting your money into the hands of what is essentially a licensed sales representative who is only trained to sell financial products. When you are sick you see a doctor, not a drug dispenser. You should also be aware of some of the practices of the existing financial distribution system. The transaction oriented financial institutions and their financial advisors depend on transactions to generate commission income. This can lead to the promotion of products that aren't the best fit for you. For the best advice, seek the help of a qualified financial advisor and for a higher level of security, consider recruiting the help of asset protection to get the most from what you earn.

The Role of the Financial Planner in Retirement Planning

A Financial Planner can offer you guidance when you are planning for one of life's major financial episodes. There is so much to navigate when planning for retirement, so having an experienced advisor is of great value. Here's why.

A Financial Planner can:

- help you find the balance between **needs, values, and desires**

- ensure that you operate within **legislative constraints** /compliance

- call your attention to **practical considerations**

- see that your level of risk is appropriate to your situation, using his **ability to project into the future**

- be of great benefit to you because through training and experience he is able to **analyze outcomes**

Just as you visit your family physician for an annual health check-up, you should demand periodic financial check-ups. Get a financial report at least once a year from your financial planner or advisor and do the same when you experience significant financial changes. You pay for his or her service either directly or indirectly, so take advantage of your entitlement to remain informed.

The Golden Years

Dignified retirement is still a cherished part of the North American dream, but for some that dream is only a fantasy. For more and more people the dignified retirement earned from a lifetime of honest work that is depicted in such movies as *On Golden Pond* is not a realistic possibility. In fact, for many, life promises no retirement at all!

We have come to expect that, when their working days are over, they can look forward to retirement. It is understood as a time to relax and enjoy the leisure they've earned after years of labour. Unfortunately, these expectations are beginning to seem unrealistic for many. Canada's pension and retirement-income system is in a shambles, and with a growing number of Baby Boomers reaching retirement age, the stage is set for a crisis of poverty among senior citizens.

The figures speak for themselves. According to investment industry analysts, North Americans are currently on track to replace less than 50% of their pre-retirement income once they retire. A rickety retirement system means more workers have to keep working. More and more people aged 65 and above are working at places like McDonald's, Tim Horton's, and Wal-Mart.

Currently, only 5% of retirees have sufficient retirement assets to realise the *On Golden Pond* dream. Unfortunately, 75% of workers don't have employer defined pension benefit plans, so they are left to fend for themselves when addressing their retirement needs. Of the employer pension plans, only public sector plans are considered to be safe due to the enshrined taxing power of the government. The majority of private sector plans are underfunded and owe billions in deficits. Consider previous Nortel employees; retirees with the Nortel Pension Plan will only get about 50% of their pension benefit entitlement. This is a very realistic possibility for many companies' employees. General Motors & Chrysler retirees, who are members of the Auto Workers' Unions, were lucky. They were saved by billions of dollars from government bailouts. But this, of course, is not always the case.

54

Alarmingly, in Canada **only 7%** of workers fully utilized the RRSP contribution room available to them. According to 2007 Stats Canada reports, the median RRSP asset per contributor is only **$2,780**! That's enough **to last for one month during retirement**. This should probably not come as a shock. The saving rate in Canada has been in negative territory for many years because people have gotten into the habit of spending more than they earn. If we maintain habits like these, the refrain, "I can't retire, I have to work" is going to become very familiar. For most people, the day they had hoped to retire will be just another day working at a desk job, cleaning, guarding, washing dishes, or greeting customers in a low-paying retail job.

The Retirement system

Canada's retirement-income system rests on what has become known as the "Three Pillars." These pillars include: Public pensions (the Canada Pension Plan and Old Age Security), workplace pensions offered by employers, and individual savings.

Unfortunately, the second pillar – workplace pension – has been in decline for the last two decades. During this period, a growing number of companies have decided that they are no longer willing, or able, to bear the cost of providing retirement income for their employees.

Since pension experts agree that in order to retire without a decrease in living standards requires an income of about 70% of pre-retirement earnings drawn from retirement savings, it's clear that North Americans are going to face serious problems when they reach the end of their working lives.

Why this shortfall?

A good workplace pension is an efficient and cost-effective way to save for retirement, but according to Canadian government figures, in 2008 only 25% of Canadian workers belonged to an employer sponsored defined pension plan. This decrease in pension coverage means workers need to take their retirement planning into their own hands.

The alternative to an employment-based pension is, of course, individual saving through a tax-exempt Registered Retirement Savings Plan. Unfortunately, the evidence suggests that registered retirement savings accounts simply aren't getting the job done for most people.

There are several reasons for this. Faced with stagnating real income and the reality of financial ups and downs, few working people are able to make regular contributions at a level high enough to generate the savings needed to support retirement. Even for those able to keep up their contributions, it's hard to invest these savings in a way that generates a reasonable rate of return, especially when stock markets are as volatile as they have been in recent years.

For these and other reasons, RRSPs just aren't cutting it. A Statistics Canada study published last year shows that, of the families whose main income earner is in the 54-to-65 age group (on the verge of retirement) only 65% have RRSP savings, and the median value of these RRSP savings is just $55,000. Those savings can't provide a dignified retirement for anyone.

Government leaders and pension advocates have admitted these problems, and various remedies have been proposed. Most recently, the government has begun to explore a new supplemental pension plan. While this proposal represents an honest attempt to address the looming crisis in retirement incomes, the design of the proposed pension is fundamentally flawed, and will not be able to solve the current problem. This is because the proposed pension suffers from some of the same problems that have hampered individual RRSPs. Even though mandatory participation is the only way to guarantee that most workers will actually get a pension, participation will not be required. The plan's proposed design also exposes individual participants to the risks of falling financial markets and low interest rates (lower interest rates make saving for retirement more expensive). Finally, the suggested contribution rates (essentially, the rate at which participants will save for retirement) are much too low to provide sufficient pension income.

Plan for a Comfortable Retirement

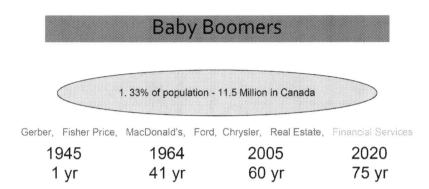

Baby Boomers

1. 33% of population - 11.5 Million in Canada

Gerber, Fisher Price, MacDonald's, Ford, Chrysler, Real Estate, Financial Services

1945	1964	2005	2020
1 yr	41 yr	60 yr	75 yr

By 2020, 1/3 of the population will be from the baby boomer generation (this encompasses every person born between 1945 and 1964).

If you want sufficient assets for a comfortable retirement, you need to start planning now. Some experts predict that you will need to be able to withdraw 60-75 % of your present income once you stop working if you want to enjoy a similar lifestyle after you retire. You'll need to save even more if you want to travel or take up expensive hobbies. But ultimately, you are the best judge of your retirement needs. Only you know what kind of lifestyle you intend to lead. With that in mind, you need to understand that you will require a retirement income stream for at least two decades. According to current projections, a 65 year old man can expect to live to age 81 and a 65 year old woman can expect to live to 84. Of course, it's impossible to know how long you'll need to support yourself, so it's best to plan for longer.

Retirement requires that you choose one of two unpleasant options: "The Pain of Change" or "The Pain of Regret"

• The Pain of Change: Embarking on retirement planning means that you'll have to make changes to your current spending behaviour and saving habits. Retirement planning requires sacrifice, discipline, and perseverance. If you can commit to these changes now, you will reap the benefits in your old age.

- The Pain of Regret: You can choose to do nothing and strive only to maintain the status quo. But you have to recognise that such a choice guarantees that you will end up living at the poverty level.

Unfortunately, too many people are counting on the solutions of yesterday to address the retirement needs of tomorrow. When you read about the problems with the following options, you'll understand how misguided beliefs can leave you stranded.

Employee pension plans: The threat of company bankruptcy makes many employees' retirement plans vulnerable. Companies might leave unfunded pension liabilities or even attempt to collapse their pension plans. Your company pension plan may not be as secure as you think. Many companies are switching from defined *benefit* pension plans, in which they assume the risk of funding a guaranteed pension amount, to defined *contribution* plans which make employees take the investment risk.

Home equity: This may not be the answer either. If you wish to continue living in your home, you may not want to suffer the erosion of estate value that a reverse mortgage would create (up to 40% of home value). If you decide to downsize and move to a smaller house, your home might generate 3-5 years of retirement income. That's a lot less than the 20 plus years you should save for to ensure that you are taken care of. The truth is your home won't help you in the long term. You can't use a roof tile or brick as currency at the grocery store so you can buy food.

The Canada Pension Plan and Old Age Security: These resources are not intended to meet retirees' full income needs. Although spouses who each receive the maximum C.P.P. and O.A.S. payments might get by if they have modest retirement expenses, the spouse who is left behind would not be able to meet all income need with a reduced pension. The *maximum* C.P.P. and O.A.S. monthly payments for 2010 are $934.17 and $516.96, respectively.

So where should you turn for financial security? Those who are smart are heading toward comfortable retirements by supplementing their private and government pension expectations with both registered and non-registered investments.

How much do you need to save to reach your retirement goals? The short answer is, as much as possible. A Financial Planner can take you through the calculations once you provide the necessary details.

The earlier you get started and the more you contribute the better. Here is some math to demonstrate why.

Starting age	25	35	45
Retirement Assets at 65 (Return on Investments = 8% per year)	$980,000	$980,000	$980,000
Retirement Income Per year	$40,000	$40,000	$40,000
Required Investment per month	$ 300	$700	$1,700

There's another benefit to contributing regularly. Contributing to investments regularly not only guarantees an ongoing savings plan for your retirement, it also evens out the risks of interest rate fluctuations and averages out the costs of shares in equity markets through dollar cost averaging.

Now that you are familiar with some of the rewards of investing, start earmarking a manageable percentage of your own income to go directly into your registered retirement savings account. Do it right away, and make it automatic. Aim to "pay yourself" 10-15 % of your income and treat it as you would any other bill. You owe that much to yourself. Most financial institutions will let you make monthly (or more frequent) contributions to an investment, RRSP, or 401k plan as an automatic withdrawal from your bank account. You won't spend what you don't see! And once you're in the habit of saving regularly you won't even miss that money. Your retirement fate is in your hands, so take control of your future before it's too late.

Top 9 retirement Savings Tips

They say a cat has 9 lives. Your RRSP may not be so lucky, but there are things you can do to make sure it thrives. Here are the 9 retirement saving tips that are crucial to achieving your financial goals.

1. Maximize your RRSP contribution
Ideally, you should meet your annual allowable contribution limit. Unfortunately, 93% of people do not maximize their RRSP contribution rooms.
Here are two ways you can make sure you use your full allowable contribution room:
- Transfer non-registered investments, such as Mutual Funds, ETFs, and Stocks, to your RRSP
- Take out an RRSP loan: The long term growth far outweighs the cost of interest. Also, you can pay down your loan and keep interest costs to a minimum with your tax refund.

2. Plan for taxes through spousal RRSPs
Spousal RRSPs are a good income splitting strategy if you expect one spouse to be in a lower tax bracket during retirement. An additional benefit is that the older spouse in a marriage can continue to make RRSP contributions to the spousal plan until the end of the year that the younger spouse turns 71.

3. Contribute early
Procrastination is costly. The sooner you contribute to your RRSP, the sooner the money can start working for you on a tax-deferred basis and the sooner you will have your tax refunds.

4. Reduce taxes withheld by your employer
A tax refund is not free money from the government, as many would like to think. Receiving a tax refund means that you have overpaid your tax obligations to the government. By filing a T1213 form to the Canada Revenue Agency, you could reduce your employer's deductions, putting more money into your pocket for immediate use.

5. Seek the advice of a tax accountant to make a tax-efficient RRSP
   deduction
You can make an RRSP contribution now and not claim the
deduction until you're in a higher tax bracket. For example, a $1,000
contribution at a 45% tax rate will generate $450 in tax savings.
Compare this to $290 at a 29% tax rate. You still benefit from the tax
deferred growth of your RRSP even if you have not taken the
deduction.

6. Know that growth is the key to your wealth creation
Many investors simply do not understand that inflation can erode the
purchasing power of money; they limit themselves to fixed income
investments such as GICs, whose returns are below the rate of
inflation. The key to achieving financial goals is a properly balanced
portfolio with equity investments that provide long-term growth
potential.

7. Avoid dipping into your RRSP prior to retirement
   Early withdrawals attract tax at your marginal tax rate. This
   means your money will be taxed when you are likely in a higher
   tax bracket than you will be when you retire. Also, you cannot
   restore RRSP contribution room. Most people don't realise that
   the RRSP room in your lifetime is limited; a withdrawal erodes
   some of this potential. The only exceptions are the "Home
   Buyers' Plan" and the "Lifelong Learning Plan." These allow
   tax-free withdrawals with the ability to re-contribute. However,
   even with these plans you cannot regain the tax-deferred growth
   on your investments that was lost.

8. Take advantage of tax-efficient investing
Capital gains and Canadian dividends are subject to a lower rate
than other sources of income, such as interest. Therefore, it makes
tax sense to hold interest-bearing investments inside your RRSP —
since they are 100% taxable anyway and hold investments that
produce Canadian dividends and capital gains outside of your
RRSP.

9. Make use of special RRSP deductions

There are two special RRSP deductions that allow you to invest more than your allowable RRSP contribution room, namely:

- Retiring allowance – If you leave a long-term employment position and receive a severance or retiring allowance, you are entitled to transfer tax-free into your RRSP an amount equal to $2,000 for each year of service before 1996; and an additional $1,500 for each year before 1989 in which you did not earn a vested pension benefit.
- Pension Adjustment Reversal (PAR) – Individuals who leave a company pension plan or deferred profit sharing plan will receive a "Pension Adjustment Reversal" if the total value of their past Pension Adjustments exceeds the benefit they receive out of the plan. The PAR restores lost RRSP contribution room.

One thing I'd like you to consider:

TFSA over RRSP

	TFSA Advantages	RRSP Disadvantages
Contribution Room	$5000 with indexed increase per year	
Cost of buying room	$0 (zero)	MTR from 21.06 to 50%
Tax efficiency	100% Tax free	Tax Deferral
Indirect Costs	No CPP contribution	CPP contribution to YMPE

The only advantage that the RRSP offers is contribution room of up to a maximum of $22,000 for 2009. But only 7% of Canadians maximize their RRSP contributions.

It's also worth considering how much you pay in extra taxes and CPP to qualify for RRSP contribution room

Pre-Retirement Process

Today, as people grow older, they enjoy healthier, actively engaged lives. As a result of healthier lifestyles, they tend to live longer as well. For all these reasons it is incredibly important to plan and save for retirement. The transition to retirement is bound to be one of the most significant lifestyle changes you'll experience, and the amount of money you save will largely define the next phase of your life. Having enough savings to live comfortably will allow you to continue to live fully. But money is not the only thing to consider. Too often, retirement planning is thought of only in terms of financial matters. While it is true that achieving financial comfort is important, a successful and fulfilling retirement experience requires planning and preparation in all areas of life.

Will you be ready?

Retirement is much more than an economic event – it is a life event that involves significant personal issues and opportunities. In fact, retirement is high on the list of the top ten life events with the most emotional impact. Among other things, you'll need to begin structuring your own activities, maintaining a network of both old and new friends, finding new interests, and sustaining your health. Today's retirees don't want to retreat from life when they leave their formal careers; they want a fulfilling lifestyle, not just rest.

Planning ahead

Getting ready for the new "after-work" phase of your life should not be a last-minute effort. Now is the time to start taking the necessary steps to build your retirement. It's your life, so you can define your priorities. But you'll need help, advice, and support from family and friends, and especially your financial advisor. You'll want to make sure your retirement dreams can be fully realised, rather than out of reach.

Personalized Retirement Plan

Every person has unique circumstances and a personal retirement goal. It is crucial that you work with your financial planner to determine how much money you'll need to support your new life. This important planning begins with a discussion around five key questions:

1. What should your income be? The rule of thumb is about 70 to 80 per cent of your current household income to maintain your lifestyle in retirement. But you may need more or less, depending on your personal retirement goals.

2. Is your current investment plan doing enough to support the retirement you want? The money you are saving through a combination of RRSPs, employer-sponsored plans, and other non-registered investments has to create an adequate retirement income after adjusted for inflation and the potentially expanding costs of health care as you age.

3. What's the best way to withdraw your money during retirement? To protect you from outliving your savings, you'll need a withdrawal strategy to help ensure that you'll have a steady income stream throughout your retirement.

4. How can you make your retirement life simpler? As you move toward retirement, your financial planner can develop strategies to simplify the administration of your assets by consolidating your various investments, savings accounts, registered plans, and insurance plans as much as possible.

5. Is your financial safety net strong enough? With age, everyday medical expenses for prescriptions and other health care necessities will rise. You may encounter an illness or injury that requires expensive home care or an extended stay in a health care facility. Any number of conditions could quickly erode your finances, so you will need to consider protecting your income with such lifestyle insurance options as critical, disability, and long-term care insurance.

Once you answer the questions above, and plan accordingly, you will be on the road to a comfortable retirement.

Trusts and Estate Planning

A trust is a relationship between three parties, in which one person (the settlor or donor) transfers assets to another person (the trustee) for the benefit of a third person (the beneficiary). The trustee manages the assets for the benefit of the beneficiary. By making this transfer, the ownership and management of the assets are separated and removed from the donor. Therefore, a trust is a means to separate the legal ownership and management of assets from the beneficial interests in the assets.

Elements of a Trust

There are three elements required to create a trust. There must be certainty of:

1. The intent of the settlor to create a trust

2. The identity of the property that is to be placed in the trust

3. The identity of the beneficiary or beneficiaries of the trust

The names of the beneficiaries may or may not be specified; they might be referred to as a class. For example, "the children" of an individual would be sufficient to satisfy the third element of a trust.

Trusts are tools that help transfer assets, but they are not separate legal entities. For tax purposes the Income Tax Act recognizes trusts as individuals for the calculation of income taxes. The trustees are the registered owners of the property within a trust; as such they are the ones who must be described as the relevant parties to any agreements.

Trusts can be used in situations in which the beneficiary is unable to enter into contracts or the settlor is not certain that the beneficiary can effectively deal with the problems associated with managing the assets. For example:

-A set of assets may be placed into a trust for a minor child. The child cannot legally enter into a contract but the trustee may do so on behalf of the child.

-A surviving spouse may not be able to manage a large and sophisticated investment portfolio or business. The assets can be placed into a trust for the benefit of the surviving spouse and managed by a trustee with the skills to handle such a portfolio.

Because the trust enables the separation of ownership and beneficial interest in a set of assets, it can be used in these situations.

What Are Estates?

An estate is made up of an individual's personal property and possessions, whether the individual is alive or deceased. During your lifetime, the management of your estate is in your care; after you pass away, your estate is administered by your executor. Conversely, a trust deals with assets that are no longer owned by the individual. It can be confusing to know which applies to what because the Income Tax Act refers to estates and trusts interchangeably.

There are two types of personal trusts referred to in the Canadian Income Tax Act: Testamentary trusts and inter vivos trusts (inter vivos literally means "among the living"). Testamentary trusts take effect after the death of an individual. Inter vivos trusts are any other personal trusts. It is important to note, however, that upon the death of the settlor, an inter vivos trust does not become a testamentary trust.

All forms of personal trusts fall within either the testamentary or inter vivos category. A spousal trust or a trust established for a child's education can be testamentary or inter vivos, but other forms of trusts might only be inter vivos.

Taxation of Trusts

You have to file a return if income from the trust property is subject to tax, in the tax year that the trust:

- has tax payable;

- is a Canadian resident and has either disposed of, or is deemed to have disposed of, a capital property or has a taxable capital gain;

- is a non-resident throughout the year, and has a taxable capital gain or has disposed of taxable Canadian property;

- is a deemed to be a resident trust;

- holds property;

- has provided a benefit of more than $100 to a beneficiary for upkeep, maintenance, or taxes for property maintained for the beneficiary's use ; or

- receives from the trust property any income, gain, or profit that is allocated to one or more beneficiaries, and the trust:

  o has a total income from all sources of more than $500;

  o has an income of more than $100 that is allocated to any single beneficiary;

  o has made a distribution of capital to one or more beneficiaries; or

  o has allocated any portion of the income to a non-resident beneficiary

Tax year

Inter Vivos Trust

ITA 108 (1) defines an inter vivos Trust as any trust other than a testamentary trust.

The tax year-end for an inter vivos trust is December 31, except for mutual fund trusts for which the year-end is December 15.

Testamentary Trust

A testamentary trust is established by the death of an individual.

The tax year-end for a testamentary trust may be December 31, but this is not a requirement. The first tax period of the trust begins the day after the donor dies, and ends at any point the beneficiary selects within the next 12 months. Both the tax rates used and the tax year of the slips issued to the beneficiary are based on the year-end of the trust.

It might be more convenient to choose a December 31 (calendar) year-end for a testamentary trust for several reasons:

- **Availability of forms** - The current-year trust returns and related schedules are usually not available until the end of the calendar year. A 2009 return due before the forms are available would have to be filed using a 2008 form, which might not contain changes or information for the current year.

- **Easier form completion** - Generally, it is easier to complete forms and interpret rules when the tax year coincides with the calendar year.

- **Availability of information** - Most information slips for income amounts are issued for the calendar year (a T5 slip for bank interest, for example).

- **Minimum delay in assessing the return** - Changes to the law generally necessitate changes to the processing procedures for a return. If the return has a tax year ending early in the calendar year, it might be necessary to delay the return assessment until the law has passed and the new procedures are in place.

However, there might also be advantages to choosing a **non-calendar** year-end. Elections to transfer certain estate losses incurred and certain gains realized on employee security options during the first tax year of the trust to the deceased person's return for the year of death, and the timing of income receipts, might play an important role when you choose the trust's tax year.

Once you establish the trust's year-end, you **cannot** change it without approval.

Allocations and designations

Generally, income is allocated to the trust's beneficiary according to the terms of the will or trust document. Depending on the type of income allocated, you might then designate all or part of the allocated amount. When you designate an amount to a beneficiary, the type of income does not lose its identity. This can allow the beneficiary to take advantage of a deduction or credit that applies to that income (such as the capital gains deduction or the dividend tax credit).

You can choose to designate the following types of income to a beneficiary:

- net taxable capital gains

- certain lump-sum pension incomes

- dividends from taxable Canadian corporations

- foreign business income

- foreign non-business income

- pension income that qualifies for the pension income amount

- pension income that qualifies for an eligible annuity for a minor beneficiary

- retiring allowances that qualify for a transfer to a registered pension plan (RPP) or a registered retirement savings plan (RRSP)

Income to be taxed in the trust

You can choose to report income on the trust return, rather than report it through the beneficiaries, as long as the trust is:

- resident in Canada throughout the year;

71

- not exempt from tax; and

- not a specified trust

This applies to income paid or payable to beneficiaries.

You can indicate this choice on line B of the return for the year that you are making a designation. Once you make this choice, you cannot deduct the income designated in the election on line 47. As an example, you might use this designation in a year in which a trust has taxable income and a non-capital loss carry forward.

Once you make this choice, you have to make it for each beneficiary. It reduces a beneficiary's income from the trust by that beneficiary's proportionate share of the income reported on the trust's return.

You can make a similar designation if taxable capital gains are included in the income reported on the trust's return. This will reduce the beneficiary's taxable capital gains from the trust, proportionate to that beneficiary's share of taxable capital gains reported on the trust's return. You might want to make the designation, for example, when you are able to use the trust's non-capital loss or net capital loss carry forward to absorb the current-year taxable capital gain.

Generally, designated amounts will reduce the adjusted cost base of a beneficiary's capital interest in the trust unless the interest was acquired for no consideration and the trust is a personal trust.

If you choose to designate any portion of the beneficiary's income to be reported on the trust return:

- enter the amount on line B of the return; and

- attach a statement to the return indicating the income you are designating and the amounts you are designating for each beneficiary

Income Attribution

Income splitting is the act of loaning or transferring money to a lower-income person (for example, a spouse or child) so the income or gains made from investing are taxed at a lower tax rate. This decreases the overall tax burden of the family unit.

Income attribution rules generally prevent attempts to shift income to another person via reattribution to the first person. However, though these rules eliminate most opportunities for income splitting, there are still a few opportunities left within a family. These are covered below.

Income on income (secondary income)

The attribution rules apply to income from property that is transferred or loaned. If this income is reinvested by the transferee or borrower, it will earn a secondary stream of income. This "secondary income" is not reattributed to the transferor or lender because it is not income from the transferred property. The transferee or borrower will be taxed for it.

It can therefore be advantageous to loan or transfer property to a spouse or minor and allow income attribution to occur on the income from the original investment. That income is then removed from the account and invested elsewhere, where it continues to earn a secondary stream of income on which no attribution occurs. A lower-income family member is taxed for this secondary income. Of course, for this to work, the loan or transfer must be legally effective.

With this type of arrangement, the key is to maintain the two accounts so that attributed income and non-attributed income are accounted for separately.

Loan for value / transfers for fair market value

If an individual makes a loan to a spouse or child, which he or she uses to invest, and interest is charged on the loan at a rate at least equal to Revenue Canada's prescribed interest rate at that time, the attribution rules will not apply. The interest, however, must be paid each year, or within 30 days after the end of the year, for the attribution rules to be disregarded. If a deadline for interest payment is ever missed, that year's income and income for all future years' will be reattributed to the lending individual.

If an individual transfers property at fair market value to a spouse or related minor child (and reports any resulting gain) and receives cash or property of equal fair market value as consideration from the spouse or child, the attribution rules will not apply. The cash or property that is given as consideration must belong to the spouse or child, and if a loan is part of this consideration it must have an interest charge, as outlined above. If the property is given to a spouse, the spouse would have to elect out of the automatic rollover, which generally makes the transfer occur at cost.

While on the surface loans for value or transfers at fair market value do not appear to achieve any income splitting gains, it might sometimes make sense to transfer property at fair market value or to loan funds and charge interest if an excess yield or capital gain can be earned. This avoids attribution and puts a high-yield asset in the hands of a lower-taxed individual. The difference between the yield and the interest charged, or the future capital gain over the fair market value transfer price, will be taxed at a lower rate. The drawback is that any interest charged on the loan is treated as income to the lender.

Loan or transfer made to earn business income

If a loan or transfer is made to earn business income (as opposed to income from property such as interest, dividends, rent, or royalties) attribution will not apply.

Your Business

When running your own business it is especially important to have a financial advisor to guide you and help you along. This section of the book focuses on Canadian policy and can get a little technical. This is merely because Canadian policy is my area of expertise. You should find this section helpful if you are entrepreneurial in spirit. The articles categorised under "Your Business" take you from the planning stages of a business to passing on the torch. For those who are wondering which businesses are most forgiving to new venturers, you'll find a couple of articles containing my advice about what to trust and what to avoid.

Consider this section your go-to guide for questions you have about business. Flip through it to brush up on your knowledge or refer to it when you need a straight-forward answer. And of course, if you need to solicit the help of a qualified financial advisor, give me a call.

The Challenges and Sacrifices of Business Ownership

Starting up your own business is an exciting dream, if you're up for the challenge. The rewards can be substantial, both financially and in terms of satisfaction when you succeed. But entrepreneurs have to be prepared for high levels of risk, lots of hard work, many great sacrifices, and a lifestyle that can be all-consuming not just for business owners, but for their families as well.

It's easy to say that entrepreneurs should tap their passions when thinking about starting a new business. After all, there's an old saying that tells us to sell what we know. But realistically, some great ideas simply don't sell and some terrible ideas do, thanks to great timing and marketing. It's a sad fact that many entrepreneurs set themselves up to fail before they even begin their exciting business ventures. These new business owners stick to bad ideas or fail to properly assess the market for a good idea. Roughly half of all new companies fail to survive during the first two years of business, and only four out of every hundred survives a decade. These are very sobering numbers. But even more worrisome is the fact that one in six successful small-business owners – the very people you'd expect to have figured it out – say they would take a pass if they had the chance to do it again.

Despite those figures, CIBC World Markets expected 150,000 Canadians to start their own enterprises before the end of 2007, adding to the 2.5 million small businesses that were already out there. This is probably because becoming a business owner is greatly valued in our society. According to a 2005 poll by Leger Marketing, more than 40% of Canadians think entrepreneurship is the most rewarding career option. Many are willing to risk their life savings – and money from their families, friends, and maybe even a bank – to take direct control of their careers. In return, they can expect to work harder and earn less than they would as corporate peons. Very few will strike it rich.

But often, opening your own business is about lifestyle choices. Sometimes people take this risk in order to pursue a lifelong dream of working in a particular field. Sometimes the desire is driven by a passion for a product, or the love of a particular working environment. Either way, it's a tough slog. But it is one that can be a lot easier with a little preparation, determination, and courage.

The key is to have a solid business plan in place so that you have some guidance and can feel a little more comfortable with your choice, having an idea of the direction your company should take. Your business plan doesn't have to be 100 pages long and it doesn't have to be prepared by an MBA, but it should indicate what the market opportunity is and should lay out how you are going to entice customers, including details about service and price. What's the compelling reason people will come to you rather than an established business? Your plan should also provide a reasonable sales forecast and an estimate of expenses. "The common rule of thumb is once you've done that, cut your sales in half and double your expenses," says Kevin Dane, vice-president and Toronto area manager with the Business Development Bank of Canada. "If it still makes sense, then maybe it's worth looking at."

Randall Craig, a Toronto management consultant and author of the 2004 book *Leaving the Mother Ship*, says committing your plan to paper reduces the likelihood that you've forgotten something. It also gives you something to show others (including your family members and business network) and helps you set financial goals that can then be tracked. "If things are going off-track, you will know about them earlier," says Craig. And chances are things will go off-track. As Dane advises, the key is to be realistic:"An entrepreneur by nature is a very optimistic person," he says, "But you have to know when to temper your enthusiasm and find a way to back up your gut feeling with some statistics."

Having relevant information at the ready will impress banks as well as franchisers. Both will also want to see up front capital. A financial institution isn't going to lend a business 100% of what it needs to start up and stay afloat. After all, banks aren't generally in the business of being shareholders. Many complain the banks aren't particularly interested in funding start-ups at all, which is perhaps one reason why 74% of Canadian respondents to a small-business survey conducted for Sage Software in 2005 reported that their enterprises were self-financed, compared to 67% North America-wide.

While entrepreneurship can be an incredibly rewarding lifestyle, it's incredibly important to consider all of the factors involved in starting your own business and to feel confident that you can succeed. Starting a business can be just as disheartening as it is exciting. Chances are you might have to fail before you succeed. But if you've got a great idea, a solid plan, and sufficient funds you might be on the track to becoming a business owner. Just be sure that you assess the risks involved.

Financial Projections and Business Plans

A business plan is a formal statement of a set of business goals that lists the reasons these goals are believed to be attainable and prescribes a plan for reaching them. It may also contain background information about the organization or team that aims to reach those goals. Business plans are decision-making tools. There is no fixed content for a business plan. Rather, the content and format of the business plan is determined by the goals and the audience. A business plan should contain whatever information is needed to decide whether or not to pursue a goal.

Preparing a business plan draws on knowledge from many different business disciplines. These include: finance, human resource management, intellectual property management, supply chain management, operations management, and marketing, among others. It can be helpful to view the business plan as a collection of sub-plans; develop one plan for each of the main business disciplines.

Financial projections are a substantial part of your business plan. Financial projections can be intimidating. However, they do not so much depend on your mathematical aptitude but, rather, on your knowledge of your business, the industry, and the market. Financial projections will attract investors and serve as a guide for future business decisions.

Financial projections require that you do the following:

- Ask people you trust in the industry to review the plan

- Match your financial forecasts against those of sample plans

- Recheck all numbers and calculations

- Look for any risks that could upset your plan

As a rule, you should always include your final financial forecasts in your business plan.

Feasibility Study

A Feasibility Study is a process that defines exactly what a project is and what strategic issues need to be addressed in order to assess the likelihood of the project's success, or its feasibility. Feasibility studies are useful when starting a new business and when identifying a new opportunity for an existing business. Ideally, the feasibility study process involves making rational decisions about a number of a project's enduring characteristics, including:

- What exactly the project is. You'll have to ask whether it is possible, it is practical, and whether it can be done.

- Economic feasibility – Are the benefits greater than the costs?

- Technical feasibility – Do you have the necessary technology? If not, can you get it?

- Schedule feasibility – Will the system be ready on time?

- Operational feasibility – Do you have the resources to build the system? Will the system be acceptable? Will people use it?

- Customer profile. This includes an estimation of customers and revenues.

- Competitive advantage. You'll need to determine where you stand in relation to your competitors.

- Current market segments. You'll need to do some research. It is important to know the projected growth in each market segment and review what is currently on the market.

- Your vision, or mission statement.

- The definition of proposed operations, management structure, and management method.

Economic feasibility

Economic analysis is the most frequently used method for evaluating the effectiveness of a new system. More commonly known as cost/benefit analysis, the procedure helps to determine the benefits and savings that can be expected from a candidate system and compares them with costs. If benefits outweigh costs, then it is feasible to design and implement the system.

Budgetary and Financial Planning For Business

Financial planning is the task of determining how a business or individual can afford to achieve his or her strategic goals. Usually, a company or individual creates a financial plan immediately after the vision and objectives have been set. The financial plan describes all of the activities, resources, equipment, and materials needed to achieve these objectives, and also determines the timeframes.

When completing your own Financial Plan, you will need to perform the following tasks:

- Assess the business environment

- Confirm the business vision and objectives

- Identify the types of resources needed to achieve these objectives

- Quantify the required resources (labour, equipment, materials)

- Calculate the total cost of each type of resource

- Summarize the costs to create a budget

- Identify any risks or issues with the set budget

A financial plan can take the form of a budget, which is an itemized estimate of spending and saving costs to be taken from your future income. Such a plan allocates future income to various expenses, such as rent and utilities, and also reserves some income for short-term and long-term savings goals. An investment plan can also serve as a financial plan; it allocates savings to various assets or projects which are expected to produce future income, such as real estate, a new business or product line, or shares in an existing business.

In business, a financial plan can also be understood to refer to the three primary financial statements (balance sheet, income statement, and cash flow statement) created as part of a business plan. Additionally, a financial forecast, or plan, can refer to a projection of the annual income and expenses for a company, division, or department. It can also be an estimation of cash needs accompanied by a method for raising money, say, through borrowing or issuing additional shares in a company.

All of these financial plans are valuable tools, and all of them can help you keep your income and expenses in order so that you can stay on the right track and meet your objectives.

Guide to Setting up a New Business
Owning Your Own Business: New, Existing, and Franchise Opportunities

There are three common ways to enter into business ownership. You may wish to start your business as a new enterprise, you could buy an existing business, or you might decide to purchase a franchise. Regardless of which type of ownership you are considering, there are some basic questions you should ask yourself to determine whether you are ready to dive in.

1. Business Planning

What Is a Business Plan?

A business plan is a recognized management tool used by successful and prospective businesses of all sizes to document business objectives and to propose how these objectives will be attained within a specific period of time. It is a written document which describes who you are and what you plan to achieve.

Why Do You Need a Business Plan?

A business plan will provide information about your proposed venture to lenders, investors, and suppliers to demonstrate how you plan to use their money and to establish the credibility of your project.

2. Organizational Structure

In Ontario there are several ways to start a business, and each structure has advantages and disadvantages. Before you decide which business form is best you, you should take into consideration personal liability, business name protection, tax advantages, and registration or filing costs.

3. Business Taxes

All businesses must be aware of the various taxes that might apply to their product or service. Depending on the location and type of products or services offered, federal, provincial and/or municipal business taxes may apply.

4. Business Regulations

Business Licenses

The Business License document is designed to provide general business licensing information for a number of specific industries and is best used as a starting point when researching regulations.

Accessibility for Ontarians with Disabilities Act

You'll need to find out how accessibility standards, under the Accessibility for Ontarians with Disabilities Act, affect businesses in Ontario. Businesses and organizations that provide goods and services to people in Ontario will have to meet certain accessibility standards in five important areas of our lives: customer service, transportation, information and communications, built environment, and employment.

Intellectual Property:

It's important to know what intellectual property covers before taking on a business venture. Intellectual property is an intangible asset that involves ideas. Some of these assets are:

- Patents

-Trade-Marks

- Copyrights

These protect your intellectual work.

Operating Your Business

The above, and the following, is by no means a comprehensive list of what to do. It will certainly be necessary to ask your [financial advisor] more questions. He or she can provide you with more detailed information about what is best for you and your business depending on your unique situation. However, a number of issues must be addressed to run the daily operations of your business. Here's a list of things you'll need to learn about:

- Bonding
- Developing New Accounts
- Selecting Professional Services
- Selecting Your Supplier
- Basic Bookkeeping
- Professional Designations
- Preventing Theft
- Setting the Right Price
- Problems in Managing a Family-Owned Business

Thinking of Retail Business? Just Say "No!"

When deciding what business to start for the first time, retail might seem like the obvious choice. Because people will always need or desire products, retail seems like a relatively safe venture. But the truth is retail is not the high value portion of the supply chain. With so much competition, you'd do best to invest in the upper end or higher value portion of the supply chain: manufacturing and wholesale distribution. When you think about some of the wealthiest people or companies in the world, the names that come to mind usually manipulate a resource and manufacture a product that is to be sold to retailers worldwide. But of those who get the product to the end user, only the big box retailers can get rich. Here are a few reasons why Mom & Pop shops can't compete.

The Competition

The mark-up retailers charge allows them to profit from the products in their stores. The mark-up is the difference between what a retailer pays for a product and the price at which the retailer sells it to customers. Though many retailers might only choose to sell products with a high retail margin, because they have to compete with big box stores they are often forced to sell for less or they are left with unsold merchandise.

Big box stores have saturated the market. These stores offer unbeatable low prices, a huge supply of products, lots of variety, and extended store hours. And because all of their locations offer these same qualities, customers know what they can expect from these stores no matter where they happen to be. This encourages loyalty to the big box name. Also, because these stores buy products in such enormous bulk quantities they get steep discounts and can afford to sell products at prices lower than the recommended retail price, consequently undercutting their competition. This makes it almost impossible for smaller competitors to survive, or even start up in a free-market economy. It doesn't help that big box stores have the space and budget to sell so many different products; with such a selection, once a customer walks in, these stores are almost guaranteed a sale! They can even tolerate the kinds of losses that smaller shops can't because it is worth it for them to stock something unprofitable just to get someone inside.

Sometimes just having an item in stock means it will yield decent profits for big box retailers. Customers are conditioned to shop at these large stores for everything from food to clothing to fishing supplies. They value the ease of a one-stop shopping trip. As they wander through the aisles customers throw more items into their shopping carts, and end up making purchases they didn't expect to make. The sheer number of items available is reason enough for customers to visit these chains, and incredible sales attract foot traffic. Often customers of smaller stores enter with a few items in mind and don't linger for hours. Smaller stores also tend to cater to one need and often can't afford to accept the losses that come with sales. Mom & Pop shops just can't compete.

What's more, internet shopping and comparison sites have created even more options than ever before, making competition especially fierce in the retail world. For all these reasons, retail is often not worth the effort. Let's consider some statistics. Historically, 50% of small start ups have failed within 2 years and 80% failed within 5 years. That means that only 20% of small start ups survive for more than 5 years. And of those, only 4% survive after 10 years! Remember, it isn't just selling products that you have to worry about; you have to consider the cost of overhead, materials, and hours (yours and your employees'). When you consider the burden that overhead costs have on an individual compared to a big box store, you'll see that the individual can't afford to sell his products for lower prices. Unfortunately this means customers will buy elsewhere.

The Truth about Franchises

Now, you might think that opening a franchise retail store is a better bet; and it is. The failure ratio is drastically reduced when entrepreneurs start their businesses with proven franchises, such as

McDonald's and Tim Horton's. But franchises come with a big price and a great sacrifice.

First of all there is a big upfront investment. This can cost anywhere from a few hundred thousand to more than a million dollars. How many people who contemplate going into the retail business have such financial resources? If you do have such resources, there are many investment options you can explore and take advantage of; you might find that other options will prove to be more profitable than becoming a franchised retail operator. One of the reasons franchisees don't earn as much as you'd expect is that royalties and fees take most of the profits earned from a franchise. Remember, you aren't the only one seeking to profit from your franchise; you have to pay your dues. You also have to keep up with the performance and appearance of all the other franchises. Many entrepreneurs don't seriously consider the hidden cost of upgrades, changes, and renovations, which franchise companies require every 5 years or so. Using the excuse of upgrades, many franchisors charge thousands, even hundreds of thousands, to replace equipment, make renovations, or change the seating arrangement at their discretion. Of course these mandatory changes are vaguely spelled out in the franchise agreements, but they can easily be missed or downplayed.

Another thing to keep in mind is your supplier. In the name of consistency, the source of supplies is mandated by the franchisors. Often the cost is higher than the cost of the same products from your neighbourhood store. The franchisors get big rebates from manufacturers and processors, but often leave you with higher costs. Technically, franchisors are supposed to share the benefits they receive from discounts with their franchisees; but in actuality this is not often the case.

So even though franchised businesses offer a good chance of success in the marketplace, the most you can earn as the franchisee is your own wages from long hours of hard work. You will likely see hardly any returns from your investment. I have seen many people invest in franchises that were not well established just because doing so was within their financial means. Most of these unproven franchises failed as fast as the Mom & Pop shops. Why would you throw away your hard earned money? If you have the money to invest, you may be better off making alternative investments in the upper portion of the supply chain with your financial resources.

Just Say "No"

It's important to understand that retailers receive a product at the end of the supply chain. Before a product hits the shelf it is sold to a distributor, then to the retailer. Both parties want to profit from the product, so there are two mark-ups required before you get to the final price – the distributor's and the retailer's. The distributor sells products at a mark-up price higher than what he paid to the manufacturer. The retailer also sells at a mark-up price, but his price is greatly influenced by the retail competition which, as described above, is pretty steep. The manufacturer and wholesaler are not affected by sales competition in the same way. The original price of the product can remain relatively constant, and if the product is popular sales are unlikely to slow down. The manufacturer and wholesaler, through distributors and retailers, also reach a much wider audience than a single retail store can, so profits are much greater.

So if you're thinking about stepping into the marketplace as a retailer, you'd do best to reconsider. In today's retail landscape, you just can't win.

Small Business Deduction
Canadian-controlled private corporation (CCPC)

For your corporation to be considered a CCPC, it must meet all of the following requirements at the end of the tax year:

- it must be a private corporation

- it must be resident in Canada; either incorporated in Canada or resident in Canada from June 18, 1971, to the end of the tax year

- it must not be controlled directly or indirectly by one or more non-resident persons

- it must not be controlled directly or indirectly by one or more public corporations (other than a prescribed venture capital corporation)

- it must not be controlled by a Canadian resident corporation that lists its shares on a prescribed stock exchange outside of Canada

- it must not be controlled directly or indirectly by any combination of persons described in the three preceding conditions

- if all of its shares owned by a non-resident person, by a public corporation (other than a prescribed venture capital corporation), or by a corporation with a class of shares listed on a prescribed stock exchange were owned by one person, that person would not own sufficient shares to control the corporation; and

- no class of its shares of capital stock is listed on a prescribed stock exchange

Small business deduction

Corporations that were Canadian-controlled private corporations (CCPCs) throughout the tax year might be able to claim the small business deduction (SBD). The SBD reduces Part I tax that the corporation would otherwise have to pay.

It is worth noting that the SBD rate has increased from 16% to 17%, effective January 1, 2008. The rate is prorated for tax years that straddle December 31, 2007.

The SBD is calculated by multiplying the SBD rate by the lowest of the following amounts:

- the income from active business carried on in Canada;

- the taxable income;

- the business limit ; or

- the reduced business limit

Active business income

Generally, active business income is income earned from a business source, including any income incidental to the business.

Income from a specified investment business or from a personal services business is generally not considered active business income and is not eligible for the SBD. The following sections explain when income from these types of businesses might be considered to be active business income and is eligible for the SBD.

Specified investment business

A specified investment business is a business with the principal purpose of deriving income from property, including interest, dividends, rents, or royalties. It also includes a business carried on by a prescribed labour-sponsored venture capital corporation, the principal purpose of which is to derive income from property.

Except for a prescribed labour-sponsored venture capital corporation, income from a specified investment business is considered to be active business income, and is therefore eligible for the SBD if:

- the corporation employs more than five full-time employees in the business throughout the year; or

- an associated corporation provides managerial, financial, administrative, maintenance or other similar services to the corporation while carrying on an active business and the corporation would have to engage more than five full-time employees to perform these services if the associated corporation were not providing them.

Note:
The business a credit union carries on, or the business of leasing property other than real property, is not considered specified investment business.

Personal services business

A personal services business is a business that a corporation carries on to provide services to another entity (such as a person or a partnership) that an officer or employee of that entity would usually perform. Instead, an individual performs the services on behalf of the corporation. That individual is called an **incorporated employee**.

Any income the corporation derives from providing the services is considered income from a personal services business, as long as both of the following conditions are met:

- the incorporated employee who is performing the services, or any person related to him or her, must be a **specified shareholder** of the corporation; and

- the incorporated employee would, if it were not for the existence of the corporation, reasonably be considered an officer or employee of the entity receiving the services

However, if the corporation employs more than five full-time employees throughout the year or provides the services to an associated corporation, the income is not considered to be from a personal services business. Therefore, the income is eligible for the SBD.

Business limit

The maximum allowable business limit for a corporation that is not associated with any other corporation is:

- $300,000 if the calendar year is 2005 or 2006

- $400,000 if the calendar year is 2007 or 2008

- $500,000 if the calendar year is 2009 or later

For tax years that straddle a calendar year, the rate is prorated based on the number of days in each calendar year.

CCPCs that are associated with one or more corporations during the tax year have to file a Schedule 23 *Agreement among Associated Canadian-Controlled Private Corporations to Allocate the Business Limit.* On this schedule, a percentage of the business limit is allocated to each corporation, and the total of all percentages cannot be more than 100%.

Large CCPCs that have taxable capital employed in Canada of $15 million or more do not qualify for the SBD. The business limit is reduced on a straight-line basis for CCPCs that have taxable capital employed in Canada in the previous year of between $10 million and $15 million. Similar restrictions apply to any CCPC that is a member of an associated group that has, in total, more than $10 million of taxable capital employed in Canada.

Manufacturing and Processing Profits Deduction

Any corporation carrying on a manufacturing or processing activity in Canada may be eligible for a tax rate reduction of 7% from 28% (federally before the surtax) to 21%. Only manufacturing and processing profits that do not qualify for the SBD (because they are in excess of the threshold or because the corporation is not a CCPC) are entitled to this tax rate reduction. In 2005, the combined federal and provincial tax rate on income eligible for this tax deduction is 34.12%.

Eligibility

To qualify as a small manufacturer, the corporation has to meet the following requirements:

1. Its activities during the year must have mainly been manufacturing or processing goods in Canada for sale or lease

2. The following calculation must total $200,000 or less: active business income minus active business losses of the corporation for the year [this includes the corporation's share of active business income and active business loss for the fiscal period of each partnership of which the corporation was a member at any time in its year]

Foreign Tax Credits for Corporations

A foreign tax credit is available to a taxpayer who is a resident of Canada at any time in a taxation year. A foreign tax credit is a deduction from the taxpayer's Canadian tax otherwise payable that may be claimed in respect to foreign **income or profits tax** paid by the taxpayer for the year. A foreign tax credit can provide relief from double taxation on certain income: i.e., relief from otherwise having to pay full tax to both Canada and another country on that income.

The taxpayer must make separate foreign tax credit calculations for:

• foreign non-business-income tax; and

• foreign business-income tax

Foreign Business Income

The total amount of a taxpayer's income from businesses carried on by the taxpayer in a particular foreign country is included in the calculation of the numerator with respect to that country. Amounts that could also be regarded as income from property are included in FBI as business income if such amounts arise from the taxpayer's business dealings in the foreign business country. FBI cannot include income business done in Canada.

Investment Tax Credits

The investment tax credit (ITC) lets you subtract, from the taxes you owe, part of the cost of some types of property you acquired or expenditures you incurred. You may be able to claim this tax credit if you bought qualifying property, incurred qualified expenditures, or were allocated renounced Canadian exploration expenses. You may also be able to claim the credit if you have unused ITCs from earlier years.

Refundable Taxes and Corporate Surplus Distributions

Generally Accepted Accounting Principles (GAAP) is the term used to refer to the standard framework of guidelines for financial accounting used in any given jurisdiction. GAAP includes the standards, conventions, and rules accountants follow when recording and summarizing transactions, and when preparing financial statements.

Corporate Surplus

Capital Dividends

The capital dividend account keeps track of various tax-free surpluses accumulated by a private corporation. These surpluses may be distributed as capital dividends free of tax to the corporation's Canadian-resident shareholders. A corporation paying a capital dividend must file an election in respect to the dividend when the dividend is paid or becomes payable. However, in certain circumstances, an election that is filed late is acceptable. If the corporation pays a capital dividend which is in excess of the balance in its capital dividend account, an additional tax may be payable on the non- qualifying portion of the dividend.

Cash Dividends

Dividends are payments made by a corporation to its shareholder members. It is the portion of corporate profits paid out to stockholders. When a corporation earns a profit or surplus, that money can be put to two uses: it can either be re-invested in the business (this is called retained earnings), or it can be paid to the shareholders as a dividend. Many corporations retain a portion of their earnings and pay the remainder as a dividend.

Stock Dividends

Stock dividends are those paid out in the form of additional stock shares from the issuing corporation, or other corporation (such as its subsidiary corporation). They are usually issued in proportion to shares owned (for example, for every 100 shares of stock owned, 5% stock dividend will yield 5 extra shares). If this payment involves the issue of new shares, it is very similar to a stock split, as it increases the total number of shares while lowering the price of each share and does not change the market capitalization or the total value of the shares held.

Dividends in Kind

Dividends in kind are those paid out in the form of assets from the issuing corporation or another corporation, such as a subsidiary corporation. They are relatively rare and most frequently are securities of other companies owned by the issuer. However, they can take other forms, like products and services.

Aggregate investment income

Aggregate investment income is defined as the following:

- Net taxable gains for the year, reduced by any net capital loss carries over deducted during the year
- Income from property including interest, rents and royalties, but excluding dividends that are deductible in computing Taxable income. Since foreign dividends are generally not deductible, they would be included in aggregate investment income.

Taxes on Dividends

The purpose of Part IV of the Income Tax Act is to prevent tax deferral on portfolio dividend income through private or closely held corporations. Corporations are generally permitted to deduct dividend income when calculating their taxable income; Part IV imposes a tax on dividends received by private corporations or closely held corporations in order to eliminate the incentive for an individual to obtain a significant tax deferral on dividend income by transferring investments in shares to such corporations. Part IV tax approximates the tax that would be paid by an individual who is taxable at the highest marginal tax rate as though the dividends had been received by that individual. Generally, this tax is fully refundable as a dividend refund to the corporation when the corporation pays dividends to its shareholders, since the shareholders will then be subject to tax at their marginal rates on the dividends.

Taxable dividends are included in the income of corporations if a corporation, which is resident in Canada, has received a taxable dividend from:

a) a taxable Canadian corporation, or
b) a corporation that is resident in Canada (other than a non-resident-owned investment corporation or a corporation exempt from Part I tax) and controlled by the recipient

Some rules allow the receiving corporation to deduct an amount equal to the dividend from income to compute its taxable income when the corporation has received a dividend from a foreign affiliate.

The Part IV tax applies to "assessable dividends" received by a corporation that was a "private corporation" or a "subject corporation" at any time during a taxation year.

An "assessable dividend" is the amount received by a corporation at a time when it is either a private corporation or a subject corporation as, on account of, in lieu of payment of, or in satisfaction of a taxable dividend from a corporation to the amount of the dividend that is deductible, when computing the recipient corporation's taxable income for the year.

Connected Corporations

Definition of "connected"

A payer corporation is "connected" with the recipient corporation at a particular time at which

a) the recipient corporation controls the payer, or
b) the recipient corporation owns, at the particular time,
   - more than 10% of the issued share capital of the payer corporation (with full voting rights under all circumstances), and
   - the payer corporation's shares with a fair market value greater than 10% of the fair market value of all the payer corporation's issued shares.

To determine whether a payer corporation is connected with a recipient corporation, subsection 186(2) of the Income Tax Act expands the normal concept of control and states that one corporation is considered to be controlled by another corporation if more than 50% of its issued share capital with full voting rights belongs to

a) the other corporation,

b) persons not dealing at arms' length with the other corporation,

or

c) the other corporation and persons not dealing at arms' length with the other corporation.

For example, consider the situation in which the issued share capital of Corporation A consists solely of 100 common shares 90 of which are owned by Mr. X. The remaining 10 common shares are owned by Corporation B, a corporation that is controlled by the spouse of Mr. X. For the purposes of Part IV, Corporation A would be controlled by Corporation B because more than 50% of the issued share capital of Corporation A is owned by Mr. X who is related to and, therefore, deemed not to deal at arm's length with Corporation B.

Dividends received from connected payer corporations

A recipient corporation is required to calculate and pay any Part IV tax by its balance-due date for its taxation year. If the recipient corporation's Part IV tax liability includes an amount calculated under tax laws, a problem may arise in which the payer corporation does not determine its dividend refund until a time that is later than the recipient corporation's balance-due date. In such situations, the recipient corporation should estimate the payer corporation's dividend refund and calculate the tax payable under Part IV. Any subsequent adjustment required, including interest, will be made on assessment. For most corporations, the balance-due date lands two months after the day that the corporation's taxation year ends; however, for certain corporations that were Canadian-controlled private corporations throughout the year, the balance-due date is three months after the day that the corporation's taxation year ends.

Refundable dividend tax on hand

The tax payable for the year under Part IV is added to the recipient corporation's "refundable dividend tax on hand" at the end of its taxation year, under paragraph 129(3)(b). Provided that the recipient corporation is a private corporation when it pays taxable dividends to its shareholders, all or a portion of the Part IV tax will be refunded to the recipient corporation as explained in the current version of IT-243, Dividend Refund to Private Corporations. By virtue of subsection 186(5), a subject corporation is deemed to be a private corporation for the purpose of the dividend refund, under section 129. The amount of a subject corporation's RDTOH is limited to the total of all taxes payable under Part IV that have not previously been refunded, whereas the RDTOH of certain private corporations (for example, a Canadian-controlled private corporation) may include other amounts.

Election to treat excessive eligible dividend designations as ordinary dividends

If you have been assessed Part III.1 tax, you can elect to treat your excessive eligible dividend designations as a separate taxable dividend in order to reduce or eliminate the Part III.1 tax otherwise payable. You may not make this election on excessive eligible dividend designations that are subject to the 30% Part III.1 tax.

To make an election you need to send a letter to your Tax Centre stating that the corporation elects in said dividend, and include the following documents:

1. If the directors of the corporation are legally entitled to administer the affairs of the corporation, a certified copy of:

a) the directors' resolution, authorizing the election to be made; and

b) the directors' declaration that the election is made with the concurrence of all shareholders who received or were entitled to receive all or any portion of the said dividend and whose addresses were known to the corporation

2. If the directors of the corporation are not legally entitled to administer the affairs of the corporation, a certified copy of:

a) the authorization of the person or persons legally entitled to administer the affairs of the corporation to make the election; and

b) the declaration of the person or persons legally entitled to administer the affairs of the corporation that the election is made with the concurrence of all shareholders who received or were entitled to receive all or any portion of the said dividend and whose addresses were known to the corporation

3. A schedule listing the following information:

a) the date of the notice of assessment of the tax that would, if not for the election, have been payable under Part III.1 of the Act

b) the full amount of said dividend

c) the date said dividend became payable, or the first day on which any part of said dividend was paid if that day is earlier

d) the portion, if any, of said dividend which is to be a separate dividend and which is a taxable dividend

Corporate Taxation and Management Decisions

Incorporate Your Small Business?

Every small business person considers whether or not to incorporate his business at some point. The form of a business isn't immutable; you can change the legal structure of your business as it grows. A common scenario is for small businesses to start out as sole proprietorships or partnerships and become incorporated once the business has grown.

If you're considering incorporating your business, here are the main advantages to incorporating.

Limited Liability

The main advantage to incorporating is the limited liability. Unlike sole proprietorship, in which the business owner assumes all liability for the company, when a business becomes incorporated an individual shareholder's liability is limited to the amount he or she has invested in the company.

If you're a sole proprietor, your personal assets, such as your house and car can be seized to pay the debts of your business; as a shareholder in a corporation, you can't be held responsible for the debts of the corporation unless you've given a personal guarantee.

A corporation has the same rights as an individual; a corporation can own property, carry on business, incur liabilities and sue or be sued.

Corporations Carry On

Another advantage to incorporating is continuance. Unlike a sole proprietorship, a corporation has an unlimited life span; the corporation will continue to exist even if the shareholders die or leave the business, or if the ownership of the business changes.

Raising Money Is Easier

Corporations also have the greater ability to raise money, which can make it easier for your business to grow and develop. While corporations can borrow and incur debt like any sole proprietorship, they can also sell shares and raise equity capital. This can be very advantageous because equity capital generally does not have to be repaid and incurs no interest. (Of course, by issuing shares, you are reducing your ownership percentage in the company.)

Income Control

If you incorporate your small business, you can determine when you receive income, which is a real tax advantage. Instead of getting your income as it's received, you can take your income at a time when you'll pay less in tax.

Potential Tax Deferral

Becoming incorporated has tax deferral potential. Because you can defer paying some tax until a later time, you may be able to realize tax savings if you are then in a lower tax bracket, or if the tax rates have fallen.

Income Splitting

Another tax advantage that comes from incorporating is income splitting. Corporations pay dividends to their shareholders from the company's earnings. A shareholder does not have to be actively involved in the corporation's business activities to receive dividends. Your spouse and/or your children could be shareholders in your corporation, which gives you the opportunity to redistribute income from family members in higher tax brackets to family members with lower incomes, who are taxed at a lower rate.

The Small Business Tax Deduction

If you incorporate your small business, your corporation may qualify for the small business deduction. This annual tax credit is calculated at the rate of 17% on the first $500,000 of taxable income (2009 or later), which may be a much lower tax rate than that applied to your personal income.

Potential Increase in Business

Having Ltd., Inc., Ltee., or Corp. as part of your company's name might increase business People tend to perceive corporations as more stable than unincorporated businesses. If you're a contractor, you might also find that some companies will only do business with incorporated companies, due to liability issues.

Section 125 of the *Income Tax Act* provides for a corporate tax reduction (commonly referred to as "the small business deduction") for CCPC income from an active business carried on in Canada. The small business deduction is provided by way of an annual tax credit, which is calculated as 17 % of the least of the corporation's:

(a) active business income for the year;

(b) taxable income for the year (subject to certain adjustments); and

(c) business limit for the year (which is generally $500,000).

The corporation must be a CCPC throughout the year to qualify for the small business deduction for that year.

The special low tax rate provided by the small business deduction recognizes the special financing difficulties and higher capital cost faced by small businesses and is intended to provide these corporations with more after-tax income for reinvestment and expansion. As the small business deduction is intended to benefit only small corporations, a large corporation's access to the deduction is restricted on the basis of its taxable capital employed in Canada.

Corporate Tax Advantages to Being a Canadian-Controlled Private Corporation

The biggest corporate tax advantage for being a Canadian-controlled private corporation is eligibility for the small business deduction described above. But there are other corporate tax advantages as well. Qualifying Canadian-controlled private corporations are also entitled to:

- an additional month to pay the balance off taxes payable under Parts I, I.3, VI and VI.1 for the year;

- enhanced investment tax credits, which may be fully refundable, for their qualified expenditures on scientific research and experimental development;

- shareholder entitlement to the capital gains exemption on the disposition of qualified small business corporation shares; and

- deferral of an employee's taxable benefits arising from the exercise of stock options granted by a CCPC (*Canadian-Controlled Private Corporation*).

Let's look at the details of some of these corporate tax advantages.

In terms of research and development expenditures, Canadian-controlled private corporations can claim federal research and development credits at a rate of 35% to reduce corporate taxes. This is a much better deal than what is available for other types of corporations, which claim a credit of 20%.

As for the "shareholder entitlement" referred to in the definition of a CCPC above, owners of shares in Canadian-controlled private corporations can claim a $750,000 lifetime capital gains exemption.

And, as Jack M. Mintz points out in "Rewarding Stagnation": "Low-taxed small business income distributed as dividends to high-income owners is typically taxed two to three and half points less than salary income. This applies to Alberta, Ontario, Nova Scotia, Prince Edward Island and Saskatchewan. (On $500,000, that translates into a tax saving of $10,000 to $16,000)

Another way of looking at the corporate tax advantages of the Canadian-controlled private corporation is to compare net corporate tax rates. For Canadian-controlled private corporations claiming the small business deduction, the net tax rate as of January 1, 2008 is 11%, while the net tax rate for other types of corporations as of January 1, 2008 is 19.5%.

As you can see, there are many advantages to being a Canadian-controlled private corporation. For more information, contact your financial advisor.

Taxable Income and Tax Payable for Corporations

Corporate income taxes

Corporate taxes include taxes on corporate income in Canada and other taxes and levies paid by corporations to the various levels of government in Canada. These include capital and insurance premium taxes; payroll levies (e.g., employment insurance, Canada Pension Plan, Quebec Pension Plan, and Workers' Compensation); property taxes; and indirect taxes, such as goods and services tax (GST), and sales and excise taxes, levied on business inputs.

Corporations are subject to tax in Canada on their worldwide income if they are resident in Canada for Canadian tax purposes. Corporations that do not reside in Canada are subject to Canadian tax on certain types of Canadian source income (Section 115, Canadian Income Tax Act).

The taxes payable by a Canadian resident corporation are determined by the corporation type:

- A Canadian-controlled private corporation is defined as a corporation that is:

- resident in Canada; either incorporated in Canada or resident in Canada from June 18, 1971, to the end of the taxation year

- not controlled directly or indirectly by one or more non-resident persons

- not controlled directly or indirectly by one or more public corporations (other than a prescribed venture capital corporation, as defined in Regulation 6700)

- not controlled by a Canadian resident corporation that lists its shares on a prescribed stock exchange outside of Canada

- not controlled directly or indirectly by any combination of persons described in the three preceding conditions. A non-resident person, a public corporation (other than a prescribed venture capital corporation), or a corporation with a class of shares listed on a prescribed stock exchange who/which owns all of its shares must not own sufficient shares to control the corporation

- not listing any class of its shares of capital stock on a prescribed stock exchange

- A private corporation is defined as a corporation that is:

- resident in Canada

- not a public corporation

- not controlled by one or more public corporations (other than a prescribed venture capital corporation, as defined in Regulation 6700)

- not controlled by one or more prescribed federal Crown corporations (as defined in Regulation 7100)

- not controlled by any combination of corporations described in the two preceding conditions

- A public corporation is defined as a corporation that is resident in Canada and meets either of the following requirements at the end of the taxation year.

- It must have a class of shares listed on a prescribed Canadian stock exchange; or

- It must have elected, or the Minister of National Revenue must have designated it, to be a public corporation. The corporation must have complied with prescribed conditions under Regulation 4800(1) for the number of its shareholders, the dispersing of the ownership of its shares, the public trading of its shares, and the size of the corporation.

If a public corporation has complied with certain prescribed conditions under Regulation 4800(2), it can elect, or the Minister of National Revenue can designate it, not to be a public corporation. Other types of Canadian resident corporations include Canadian subsidiaries of public corporations (which do not qualify as public corporations), general insurers, and Crown corporations.

Computation of Net Income

Net income is equal to the income that a firm has after subtracting costs and expenses from the total revenue. Net income can be distributed among holders of common stock as a dividend or can be held by the firm as retained earnings.

Computation of Taxable Income

Deductions available to corporations

Losses

A business loss can be carried forward for 20 years and back for three years.

Depreciation

Fixed assets generally depreciate according to the declining balance method. Rates are 10% for certain buildings, 30% for heavy construction equipment and 20% for cars and machinery.

Transfer Pricing

A transfer through a non arm's length non-resident should be the same price as an arm's length side. Companies must keep documents and file reports regarding such transactions.

Thin Capitalization

Interest paid on a loan from a related non-resident to a Canadian company is deductible only if the loan to equity ratio does not exceed a 2:1 ratio.

Consolidated returns are not allowed in Canada. Each company has to file separately.

Canada Deduction at Source

Tax withholding rates for payments to non-residents are as follows:

Dividends - 25%.

Interest - 25%.

Royalties - 25%.

Note: Rates may be reduced by double taxation treaties

Dividends

Dividend tax credit

The dividend tax credit is a non-refundable tax credit which applies when Canadian dividends are included in income. However, foreign dividends do not qualify for the dividend tax credit.

The dividend tax credit for dividends received after 2005 is dependent on the type of corporation paying the dividend. There are two types of Canadian dividends. These are usually referred to as "eligible" or "non-eligible" dividends. Most dividends received from Canadian public corporations are eligible for the enhanced dividend tax credit (eligible dividends); most dividends received from Canadian-controlled private corporations (CCPCs) are eligible for the regular or small business, dividend tax credit (non-eligible dividends).

Acquisition of Control Rules

Acquisition of control rules apply when a corporation's ability to deduct previously unutilized losses is restricted because control of the corporation has been acquired by a person or group of persons.

TAXATION YEAR END BEFORE ACQUISITION OF CONTROL

Generally, the rules in subsection 249(4) apply when control of a corporation is acquired by a person or a group of persons. However, these rules do not apply if the corporation is a foreign affiliate that does not carry out business in Canada and if control was acquired after July 13, 1990.

Subsection 249(4) states that the taxation year of the corporation is deemed to end immediately before the time that control is acquired. A new taxation year is deemed to begin at that time. This will give rise to the normal events that follow a taxation year-end, including the filing of the corporation's tax return and payment of taxes due. Starting with the new taxation year, the corporation may adopt a new fiscal period without seeking the concurrence of the Minister. When the acquisition of control occurs no more than 7 days after the end of a corporation's taxation year, however, and that taxation year did not end as a consequence of the acquisition of control or emigration, bankruptcy, or change in the tax-exempt status of the corporation, the corporation may elect in that year's tax return to extend the preceding taxation year so that it ends immediately before the acquisition of control.

RESTRICTIONS ON LOSS UTILIZATION BY A CORPORATION FOLLOWING AN ACQUISITION OF CONTROL

NET CAPITAL LOSSES

When the control of a corporation is acquired by a person or group of persons, the corporation's net capital losses for taxation years ending before control was acquired cannot be carried forward to any taxation year that ends after control was acquired. Similarly, a corporation's net capital losses incurred in a taxation year that ends after control was acquired cannot be carried to a taxation year that ends before control was acquired.

NON-CAPITAL LOSSES AND FARM LOSSES - STREAMING RULES

When the control of a corporation is acquired by a person or group of persons, the general rule is that no amount of the corporation's non-capital loss or farm loss for a taxation year that ends before the acquisition of control is deductible for a taxation year that ends after the acquisition of control.

Non-capital losses and farm losses can no longer be carried forward for deduction against taxable capital gains that arise after an acquisition of control. However, a corporation, when computing its taxable income for a particular taxation year that ends after an acquisition of control, can deduct a non-capital loss or farm loss incurred before the acquisition of control if the particular business which gave rise to the loss is carried on by the corporation for profit, or with a reasonable expectation of profit, throughout the particular year. The amount that may be deducted is the lesser of:

(a) the aggregate of

(i) that portion of its non-capital loss or farm loss for a taxation year that ends before the acquisition of control that was incurred in carrying on a business (losses attributed to property and allowable business investment losses expire); and

ii) if the loss was incurred after the 1987 taxation year and the business was carried on in that year, that portion of the loss that represents the amount that would otherwise have been deductible in computing the corporation's taxable income for the loss year

(b) the aggregate of the corporation's income for the particular year from that business and – if properties were sold, leased, rented or developed or services were rendered in the course of carrying on that business before that time – from any other business substantially, all the income of which was derived from the sale, leasing, rental or development, as the case may be, of similar properties or the rendering of similar services.

Non-capital losses and farm losses may not be carried forward to a post-acquisition of control year if the loss corporation was not, throughout that post-acquisition year, carrying on "that business." Whether the corporation carried on "that business" is a question of fact. Factors that are considered when determining whether "that business" was carried on include the following:

(a) the location of the business carried on before and after the acquisition of control

(b) the nature of the business

(c) the name of the business

(d) the nature of income-producing assets

(e) the existence of a period or periods of dormancy

(f) the extent to which the original business constituted a substantial portion of the corporation's activities in the allocation of time and financial resources

Geographical Allocation of Income

After Taxable Income is calculated, in order to determine the amount of provincial taxes that is payable and the provinces to which taxes are due, it is necessary to allocate the income of the corporation to the various provinces.

In order for a corporation to have "taxable income earned in the year in a province," it is necessary to determine whether it has a permanent establishment in that province in the year. A corporation has a permanent establishment in a province if it has a fixed place of business there. It may also have a permanent establishment in certain other circumstances, such as when it carries on business through an employee or agent, or uses substantial machinery or equipment in a province. When a corporation has a permanent establishment in a province, 10% of its taxable income earned in that province in the year may be deducted from its Part I tax otherwise payable.

Federal Tax Payable

When it comes to federal corporate rates, the basic rate of tax is 38% of your taxable income, and it is 28% after federal tax abatement.

For Canadian-controlled private corporations claiming the small business deduction, the net tax rate before surtax is 11%, effective January 1, 2008.

For other corporations, the net tax rate before surtax will decrease as follows:

* 19%, effective January 1, 2009

* 18%, effective January 1, 2010

* 16.5%, effective January 1, 2011

* 15%, effective January 1, 2012

The corporate surtax is zero, effective January 1, 2008.

Federal Tax Abatement

The federal tax abatement is a 10% reduction on the federal tax rate. It is designed to leave room for the provinces to apply their respective tax rates. It reduces the basic federal tax rate from 38% to 28%.

Provincial or territorial rates

Generally, provinces and territories have two rates of income tax - a lower rate and a higher rate.

Lower rate

The lower rate applies to either:

• the income eligible for the federal small business deduction; or
• the income based on limits established by the particular province or territory.

Higher rate

The higher rate applies to all other taxable income.

Provincial and territorial tax rates (except Quebec and Alberta)

The following table lists the income tax rates for provinces and territories (except Quebec and Alberta, which do not have corporation tax collection agreements with the CRA).

Province or territory	Lower rate	Higher rate
Newfoundland and Labrador	5%	14%
Nova Scotia	5%	16%
Prince Edward Island	3.2%*	16%
New Brunswick	5%	13%**
Ontario	5.5%	14%
Manitoba	1%	13%***
Saskatchewan	4.5%	12%
British Columbia	2.5%	11%
Yukon	4%	15%
Northwest Territories	4%	11.5%
Nunavut	4%	12%

* 2.1%, effective April 1, 2009
** 12%, effective July 1, 2009
*** 12%, effective July 1, 2009

Maximize Your Business Income Tax Deductions

The first rule for maximizing your business income tax deductions is that you must have all of your business-related receipts. The CRA (Canada Revenue Agency) and IRS (Internal Revenue Service) insist that all of your business expenses need to be backed up with receipts, so you have to collect them and keep them together. For tax purposes the CRA and IRS ask you to keep all of your receipts for six years, as the CRA or IRS might want to look at them years later.

In my opinion, keeping track of all of those receipts throughout the year is the most difficult part of preparing for your income taxes. Training yourself to always ask for a receipt, no matter how small the purchase, will get you into the habit and will ensure that you have what you need.

You should also train yourself to look at your receipts when you first collect them to make sure the receipts indicate the purchase or labour and have a legible vendor's name and date. Illegible or incomplete receipts are a nightmare when it comes to recording the receipt data into the record-keeping system you're using for accounting purposes – especially if you or your bookkeeper is trying to figure out the details of an incomplete receipt and record it months after the purchase. Getting into the habit of looking at your receipts as you collect them to make sure they are legible and contain all of the necessary information is a vital first step toward maximizing your business income tax deductions.

Tax Deductions

The cost of doing business is an important part of calculating your small business tax deductions. Use this checklist to ensure that you're maximizing your income tax deductions in this category of business expenses.

1) Have you deducted all of your business taxes, business-related dues, memberships and subscriptions?

No one forgets that business licensing fees or business taxes are an income tax deduction, but sometimes people overlook some of the annual membership dues they pay to business-related organizations. If you're like me you belong to several, so make sure you're deducting all of the appropriate fees on your income tax.

2) If you've borrowed money to run your business, have you deducted all of the interest and related fees?

Generally, the interest you pay on money you borrowed to run your business is tax deductible. You can also deduct related fees, such as fees paid to reduce the interest rate on your loan, or fees related to the purchase or improvement of a business property, if that's what the loan was for. This includes application, appraisal, and relevant legal fees. For more information about this tax deduction, see the Interest section of the CRA's Business and Professional Income Guide.

3) Have you deducted all insurance business expenses?

Although life insurance premiums aren't a permissible income tax deduction, you can deduct the insurance premiums you've paid for insurance on the building(s), machinery, or equipment you use in your business.

4) Have you deducted all management and administration business expenses?

Whatever management and administration charges you've incurred over the past year are legitimate business expenses and legitimate income tax deductions. This includes bank charges!

5) Have you deducted all relevant maintenance and repair business expenses?

You can deduct the cost of maintenance and/or repairs for the property you used to earn income over the past year. In most cases, the full cost of both labour and materials will qualify as a small business tax deduction. If you did the work yourself, you'll only be able to deduct the cost of the materials.

6) Have you deducted the full cost of all your office's business expenses and supplies?

If you have a traditional office, the cost of all those paper clips, staples, pens, and packages of computer paper can really add up over the course of a year. Depending on your business, you may also have supplies expenses. Some examples are the cost of film if you're a photographer or the cost of drugs if you're a veterinarian. Generally, supplies are defined as items consumed indirectly to provide the goods or services a business provides, and should be included in your income tax deductions.

Management Compensation (Salary and Dividends)

The federal Income Tax Act allows the deduction of expenses when calculating the taxable income from a business. Because certain expenses are not treated the same for tax purposes as they are in accounts of the business, net income, or profit, they are not necessarily the same as taxable income. Wages and salaries, and interest on borrowed money, for example, are treated the same for both tax and accounting purposes. Thus, if a business is not incorporated, the owner may take a salary that reduces the profit and bears the personal income tax.

If the business is incorporated to take advantage of the benefits of incorporation, such as limited personal liability, the owner may choose to take a portion of the profit as his or her salary and a portion as dividends, which are also subject to personal income tax. The dividends also bear corporate income tax, as noted above, so the dividend income received by the shareholder will effectively be taxed twice. To minimize this double taxation, the Income Tax Act sees that dividends from Canadian companies are grossed-up by 25% for ineligible dividend and by 45% for eligible dividend. The grossed-up amount—125 or 145 percent of the dividend actually received—is included in taxable income, and a credit equal to 13.33 or 18.96 percent of that amount is deducted as a credit from the federal tax that is otherwise payable. In theory, the remainder of the 25 or 45 percent gross-up is allowed as a credit against provincial income tax otherwise payable. In practice, as noted below, the provincial dividend tax credit varies considerably from province to province.

When the recipient is another Canadian corporation, the dividends are not included in the taxable income of the recipient company. That would lead to double corporate taxation of the dividend.

The end result is that individuals who receive dividends from small companies have almost all, and in some cases more than all, of the corporate income tax applied against their personal income tax, thereby eliminating double taxation. Because the gross-up-and-credit system allows for the pass through of the equivalent of a tax of only 20 percent on corporate income, only a part of the tax is credited for recipients of dividends from large Canadian companies.

An approximate mechanism

Not all corporations pay full income tax rates on their book profit, but the gross-up-and-credit system assumes that they do. Prior years' losses, heavy investment in new physical assets, exploration expenses in the natural resource sector, and research and development incentives, among other things, can reduce the actual tax payable to be well below the nominal rate for book profit. Despite this, the full gross-up-and-credit system applies. In these cases, the total tax on dividends could fall short of the amount that would have been payable under the other two alternatives examined below. Often, however, the differences between nominal and effective rates of tax on book profit even out over time; in later years the total tax burden on dividends may be significantly higher than shown here.

A practical example

The variation in tax burdens on different forms of income is not an abstract issue, but one that is faced by many small-business people. Consider three children in Prince Edward Island who have inherited an incorporated family firm worth $3 million. A cousin runs the firm and draws an annual salary of $50,000. Two sisters and one brother are not involved in the firm, but each is guaranteed a return of 5 percent—$50,000—on their share of the firm's profit before tax. One sister chooses dividends, the second chooses straight interest, and the brother sells the equivalent in shares to the cousin every year. After paying income tax, the siblings end up with the following amounts:

- Dividends—$35,508

- Interest—$37,179

- Capital gains—$35,188

The cousin also has to contribute to employment insurance (EI) and the Canada pension plan (CPP), and ends up with $35,301 after tax. In addition, the company has to pay $2,874, as its share of EI and CPP levies on the cousin's salary. Although the cousin's total tax burden, including the firm's EI and CPP obligations, is higher than those of the three siblings, the EI and CPP programs provide additional benefits to the cousin that are not available to the others. Furthermore, the cousin is the only one who can contribute to an RRSP.

The typical owner-manager has to decide what combination of salary, dividends, and reinvestment in the firm will produce the best after-tax return for his or her efforts. The board of directors of a large firm has to select the balance of dividends and reinvestment, both taxable and non-taxable, which will best suit the majority of their investors.

Example 1 - Dividends

	Small business $	Large business $
Corporate profit before tax	100.00	100.00
Corporate income taxes		
Federal	13.12	26.12
Provincial nominal	10.00	10.00
Net profit available for dividends	76.88	63.88
In the hands of an individual		
Grossed-up dividend	96.10	79.85
Federal income tax at top marginal rate	27.87	23.16
Federal dividend tax credit	12.81	10.64
Net federal tax	15.06	12.51
Provincial tax	13.38	11.12
Provincial dividend tax credit	6.15	5.11
Net provincial tax	7.23	6.01
Net federal and provincial tax on dividend	22.29	18.52
Combined personal and corporate income tax	45.41	54.64

[a] Assumes rate applicable for non-resident of a province

Example 2 - Wages or Salaries

Profit spent as wage to owner	All Corporations $
Corporate profit before tax	100.00
Corporate income taxes	
Federal	0.00
Provincial nominal	0.00
Available for reinvestment	100.00
Federal income tax at top marginal	29.00
Provincial income tax	13.92
Combined personal and corporate income tax	42.92

[a] Assumes rate applicable for non-resident of a province

Example 3 - Capital Gains

	Small business $	Large business $
Corporate profit before tax	100.00	100.00
Corporate income taxes		

Federal	13.12	26.12
Provincial nominal	10.00	10.00
Available for reinvestment	76.88	63.88
Capital gains realized	76.88	63.88
Amount of capital gains taxed	38.44	31.94
Federal income tax at top marginal rate	11.15	9.26
Provincial tax	5.35	4.45
Net personal income tax	16.50	13.71
Combined personal and corporate income tax	39.62	49.83

Section 85

Rollovers are transactions that defer the tax otherwise payable on dispositions of property. A disposition of property is a taxable event; any time a taxpayer disposes of property the taxpayer realizes "proceeds of disposition" for the property and must compute the gain or loss realized on the disposition, and include the result in the taxpayer's income.

Paid-Up Capital ("PUC")

Paid-up capital (PUC for short) is the shareholder capital that has been paid by shareholders in full. It is:

(a) in respect to a share of any class of the capital stock of a corporation, an amount equal to the paid-up capital at that time. In respect to the class of shares of the capital stock of the corporation to which that share belongs, it is divided by the number of issued shares of that class outstanding at that time.

(b) in respect to a class of shares, of the capital stock of a corporation.

(c) in respect to all of the shares of the capital stock of a corporation, an amount equal to the total of all amounts, each of which is an amount equal to the paid-up capital in respect to any class of shares of the capital stock of the corporation at the particular time

Notice the structure: (a) is PUC of a share; (b) is PUC of shares of a class; and (c) is PUC of shares of all classes.

PUC attaches to shares of a class, not to any shareholder (or taxpayer). PUC is computed without regard to who owns the share. This is contrasted with, for example, the adjusted cost base of a share which is computed by reference to the taxpayer.

Paragraphs (a) & (c) of the PUC definition are subject to the following qualifying statements: paragraph (c) is the sum of all classes, and paragraph (a) divides the class PUC by the number of shares in the class, to get the PUC per share.

Paragraph (b) is the heart of the PUC definition. PUC is in respect to a class of shares is PUC "without reference to the Act," except certain specific subsections, which can alter this number. Many of these subsections are part of the rollover provisions in the Act which seek to prevent PUC from being increased in the course of corporate reorganizations.

What is PUC determined "without reference to the Act"? There is no direct authority. It is commonly accepted to be the share capital of the class for corporate law purposes. Under the *Business Corporations Act* (BC) it is the "par value" of the shares issued, if the shares have par value and the consideration received by the company on the original issuance of the shares if the shares have no par value. Under the federal *Canada Business Corporations Act* (*"CBCA"*), and in provinces that use the *CBCA* as a model, such as Ontario and Alberta, it is the "stated capital" account maintained for the class, namely the consideration received on the original issuance of the shares, or a lesser amount in "non-arm's length" circumstances.

This is PUC of a class "without reference to the Act." This is the opening PUC of a class for tax purposes. It can be referred to as "corporate share capital" and is basically what the directors have recorded as the amount the corporation received on issuance of the shares (the actual amount, the par value, or possibly lower stated capital). Again, it attaches to the whole class of shares, and not to any particular shareholder. This PUC is the tax PUC, unless one of the specific sections noted adjusts this tax PUC further.

Asset Transfer: Example

Let's assume:

• Simon sells $5 million of real estate with a mortgage of $1.7 million and a cost amount of $2 million to a Canadian controlled private corporation ("CCPC") in exchange for:

– $3 million of preferred shares which will have an adjusted cost base and paid-up capital of nil;

– assumption of the $1.7 million mortgage; and – a $300,000 promissory note

• common shares of the CCPC are issued to a trust for the benefit of Simon's lineal descendants.

• 20 years later Simon dies and, immediately before that, the value of the CCPC shares is $13 million.

The result is that until such time as the CCPC sells the apartment or Simon's lineal descendants dispose, or are deemed to dispose of, their shares of the CCPC, tax of $2,185,000 on the $10 million of growth that arose after the freeze, will be deferred by virtue of the transfer. There is still tax of $655,500 on the $3 million of preferred shares received by Simon as a part of the estate freeze and deemed to be disposed of immediately before his death. Note that by transferring real estate that includes depreciable property, the potential for recaptured depreciation taxed at 43.7% has been replaced with the potential for a capital gain taxed at 21.85%.

Management Consultancy

Management consulting involves both the industry of and the practice of helping organizations improve their performance, primarily through the analysis of existing business problems and the development of plans for improvement.

Organizations hire the services of management consultants for a number of reasons. Organizations might: desire external (and presumably objective) advice; value the opportunity to have access to a consultant's specialized expertise; or simply need extra help temporarily for a one-time project, for which the hiring of more permanent employees is not necessary. Consultancies can offer ideas for organizational change, the development of coaching skills, technology implementation, strategy development, or operational improvement services and can provide management assistance.

Due in large part to their exposure to and relationships with numerous organizations, consultancies are often said to be aware of industry "best practices," but the transferability of such practices from one organization to another is a subject of debate. Management consultants generally bring their own proprietary methodologies or frameworks to guide the identification of problems and serve as the basis for recommendations of more effective or more efficient ways of performing business tasks.

Partnerships

What is a partnership?

A partnership is a business formed by two or more co-owners. Like a sole proprietorship, a partnership is easy to form. A simple verbal agreement is sufficient, but if money and property is at stake a formal agreement should be written.

There are two types of partnerships, a general partnership and a limited partnership.

General Partnership

In a general partnership, all partners share in gains and losses and all have unlimited liability for all partnership debts, not just a share of them. The partnership agreement describes the way partnership gains and losses are divided.

Limited Partnership

In a limited partnership, one or more general partners have unlimited liability and run the business for one or more limited partners who do not actively participate in the business. A limited partner's liability for business debts is limited to the amount contributed to the partnership. This form of organization is common in real estate ventures, for example.

What should be included in the partnership agreement?

The partnership agreement should outline the following: the objectives of the partnership; the investment amount from each partner; how gains and losses are divided; the duties and participation levels of partners; provisions for death, retirement, or succession; the dissolution of the partnership; and any special conditions.

Note: You might want to contact a lawyer for partnership agreements, procedures, and issues.

What are the advantages and disadvantages of a partnership agreement?

Advantages:

1. Easy set up: like a proprietorship, a partnership is easy to form.

2. Affordability: partnerships usually have low start-up costs.

3. Minimal registration requirements: you'll only need a certificate of compliance, business license, registration of business name, and GST registration.

4. Minimal government regulations: there are minimal government stipulations to follow.

5. Tax advantages: lower tax rate and losses may be applied against partners' other income.

6. Business continuity: partnership will continue until the death of one of the partners or until one of the partners decides to dissolve the business.

7. Incorporation: it isn't difficult to convert a partnership to a different business structure.

Disadvantages:

1. Unlimited liability: creditors can look beyond business assets to the partners' personal assets for payments.

2. Difficulty in finding partners: it can be difficult to find a compatible partner to do business with.

3. Difficulty obtaining start-up costs: the amount of equity that can be raised is limited to the partners' personal wealth. Due to the risk of partnerships, it is often difficult to obtain financing.

4. Employment insurance ineligibility: if the business does not succeed, the partners are not eligible to collect employment insurance benefits.

5. Tax disadvantage: profits must be added to personal income.

6. Shared control and profits: partners need to compromise and agree to mutually beneficial terms.

7. Potential for conflict: since everything is shared there is great potential for conflict.

8. Termination of business: the legal life of the business terminates with the death of a partner unless the partnership agreement states otherwise and the remaining partners decide to continue the partnership.

How does a partnership pay your taxes?

A partnership does not pay income tax on its operating profits and does not have to file an annual return by itself. Instead, each partner includes a share of the partnership income or loss on a personal, corporate, or trust income tax return. Each partner also has to either file financial statements or one or more of the following applicable forms: Statement of Business Activities (form T2124), Statement of Professional Activities (form T2032). This is necessary whether or not you actually received your share in money or in credit to your partnership's capital account.

A partnership has to a file a partnership information return if, over the fiscal period, it has six or more partners or if one of its partners is a partner of another partnership.

How does GST/HST affect a partnership?

A partnership is considered to be a separate person and must file a GST/HST return and remit tax where applicable.

Co-Ownership

Co-ownership is a legal concept according to which two or more co-owners share the legal ownership of a property. The purchaser obtains ownership of a percentage interest in the common areas of the building by a deed. He or she gains the exclusive right to occupy a specific unit through a registered Co-Ownership Agreement and the provisions of the Co-ownership Agreement. Through these measures, the purchaser becomes a member of the Co-Ownership Corporation which:

(A) Manages the affairs of the building according to the Co-ownership Agreement, the Corporation by-laws, and/or private contracts.

(B) Represents the interest of the owners.

The purchaser can individually finance his or her own unit and is assessed for a percentage share (based on the size of the unit in relation to the whole building) of common expenses. The purchaser is subject to the Co-Ownership Agreement Rules and By-Laws and to the Co-Ownership Corporation's other contractual documents. For example, the Co-Ownership Agreement requires the establishment of a reserve monetary fund for building maintenance. In return, the purchaser can participate in management decisions by sitting on the Board of Directors and voting at annual General meetings.

Joint Venture

A joint venture is an entity formed between two or more parties that allows them to undertake economic activity together. To create a new entity, each party must contribute equity; they then share in the revenues, expenses, and control of the enterprise. The venture can be for one specific project or for a continuing business relationship, like the Fuji Xerox joint venture. This is in contrast to a strategic alliance, which involves no equity stake by the participants, and is a much less rigid arrangement.

The phrase 'joint venture' generally refers to the purpose of the entity and not to a particular type of entity. Therefore, a joint venture may be a corporation, limited liability Company, partnership, or other legal structure, depending on a number of considerations such as tax and tort liability.

Partnership Income and Losses

A partnership is not deemed to be a person. However, when determining a member's share of a partnership's income or loss from a source or sources in a particular place, the partnership first computes its income as though it is a person. A member's share of the income or loss from each source then flows through to him, retaining its characteristics in respect to its source and nature.

When determining income or loss at the partnership level, capital cost allowance on property owned by the partnership and various reserves permitted by the Act are claimed by the partnership, not by the partners individually.

Dividends

The income or loss allocated to each partner is his share of the net income or net loss (after applicable expenses) from any source or from sources in a particular place. However, when a partnership receives dividends from a taxable Canadian corporation, and there are expenses applicable thereto, it is considered that the partnership may allocate to each member his share of the gross dividend and his share of the expenses. The effect is that the gross-up of the dividend and the dividend tax credit are calculated on the gross dividend rather than on the net dividend income.

Partnership income from a particular source retains its identity in the hands of a partner. Therefore, to the extent that the income from a particular source qualifies, the partner is entitled to take advantage of the transitional averaging provisions.

End of Fiscal Period

Assume a partnership (the first partnership) is a member of another partnership (the second partnership) which ceases to exist before the end of its normal fiscal period; the first partnership cannot use this same option. For example, suppose that the fiscal period of the first partnership ended on December 31, 1972. The fiscal period of the second partnership ended on June 30, 1972. If the second partnership ceased to exist on October 31, 1972, the first partnership includes in income for the 1972 taxation year its share of the income of the second partnership for the periods ending June 30, 1972 and October 31, 1972. The first partnership cannot use subsection 99(2) to move back the end of the second period from October 31, 1972 to June 30, 1973.

Salaries

Salaries paid by a partnership to its members do not constitute a business expense, but are a method of distributing partnership income among members. The income of a partnership in a taxation year might be less than the partner salaries indicated by the partnership agreement. In this event, the excess over the income would appear as a deduction in the partners' capital accounts. Such a reduction of each partner's capital is permitted as a deduction to determine the allocation to him of the income or loss of the partnership.

Limited Partnerships

A limited partnership is a form of partnership similar to a general partnership, except that in addition to one or more general partners (GPs), there are one or more limited partners (LPs). It is a partnership in which only one partner need be a general partner.

The GPs are, in all major respects, in the same legal position as partners in a conventional firm, i.e. they have management control, share the right to use partnership property, share the profits of the firm in predefined proportions, and have joint and several liabilities for the debts of the partnership.

Like shareholders in a corporation, LPs have limited liability, meaning they are only liable on debts incurred by the firm to the extent of their registered investment and have no management authority. The GPs pay the LPs a return on their investment (similar to a dividend), the nature and extent of which is usually defined in the partnership agreement.

Limited partnerships are distinct from limited liability partnerships, in which all partners have limited liability.

Limited Partner's Share of Limited Partnership's Loss

The Department considers that a limited partner's share of a partnership's loss cannot exceed the lesser of his share of the partnership's loss, as determined by the provisions of the relevant Partnership Act or the agreement between all members of the partnership, and his "equity" in the partnership determined as the aggregate of the capital he has contributed and any amount he has agreed to pay to the partnership as an additional capital contribution plus or minus the net adjustments to the adjusted cost base of his interest in the partnership. Any loans or advances made to the partnership by a limited partner and any obligations of the partnership guaranteed by a limited partner are not considered to be an addition to partnership "equity."

Transfer of property or services for a partnership

Partners can generally transfer property into and out of partnerships without recognizing gains or losses on the transfers. A distributing partner typically recognizes a gain only when the cash receipts exceed the outside basis. Distributing partners never recognize losses on ordinary partnership distributions. By allocating gross income to a partner providing property or services with a useful life extending beyond the end of a taxable year, partnerships can gain the equivalent of current deductions for capital expenditures. Generally, the substance of the transaction decides whether the partner realizes a gain on a transfer of property to a partnership.

A partnership distribution can be in the form of cash, property, or a combination of the two. Cash distributions can be either actual or constructive. The distribution can be either current or liquidating. The ultimate cash distribution relating to a partner's distributive share is generally not considered taxable income under the aggregate approach to partnership taxation because the partner is taxed on his distributive share of partnership income. A liquidating distribution is like a current distribution, as the gain is only recognized when the distribution exceeds the basis of the partner's interest. However, a limited loss can be recognized in a liquidating distribution.

Partnerships and GST

From a structural perspective, the GST legislation is strikingly different from the Income Tax Act in its treatment of partnerships. For GST purposes, partnerships are defined as separate "persons" which can create some difficulties in even the most common income tax transactions. ETA section 272.1 is meant to provide a statutory codification of the way in which partners are seen to interact with their partnership entities for GST purposes. There is a broad deeming rule: "anything done by a person as a member of a partnership is deemed to have been done by the partnership in the course of the partnership's activities and not to have been done by the person".

The subsection 272.1(1) deeming rule has broad application and is significant when partners provide goods, services, or employment labour to their partnerships. In the absence of some certainty about how transactions between partners and their partnership entities are treated, the "first principles" conclusion is that the GST applies. For example, if a partner is reimbursed for the purchase of a new computer for her law firm, is the partner required to register, charge, and collect GST on the reimbursement? Subsection 272.1(1) is not likely to apply in this case, but might apply in many similar examples in most corporate commercial transactions involving partnerships. If a limited partnership is created, and one partner provides some goods and management services while another contributes the labour of its employees, it is not clear whether the partners must charge GST to the partnership. Furthermore, it is not clear who is entitled to claim the ITCs that may have been paid by the partners on the initial acquisition of the goods or services. This is a significant question, particularly if the partnership entity is engaged in exempt activities and unable to recover any GST charged. In one recent situation, $11 million a year was at issue, and any GST payable by the partnership was not recoverable because it was engaged in an exempt business.

Business Valuation and Buying or Selling an Incorporated Business

The Valuation of a Business

Business valuation is a set of procedures used to estimate the economic value of an owner's interest in a business. Valuation is used by financial market participants to determine the price they are willing to pay or receive to consummate the sale of a business. In addition to estimating the selling price of a business, the same valuation tools are often used by business appraisers to resolve disputes related to estate and gift taxation and divorce litigation, or to allocate the business purchase price among business assets, establish a formula for estimating the value of partners' ownership interest for buy-sell agreements, and fulfill many other business and legal needs. Following is a list of methods used for business valuation.

Adjusted Book Value: This is one of the least controversial valuation methods. It is based on the assets and liabilities of the business.

Asset Valuation: This is often used for retail and manufacturing businesses because they have a lot of physical assets in inventory. Usually it is based on inventory and improvements that have been made to the physical space used by the business. Discretionary cash from the adjusted income statement can also be included in the valuation.

Capitalization of Income Valuation: This is frequently used by service organizations because it places the greatest value on intangibles, giving no credit for physical assets. Capitalization is defined as the Return on Investment that is expected. In a nutshell, one ranks lists of variables with a score of 0-5 based on how strong the business is in each of those variables. The scores are averaged for a capitalization rate which is used as a multiplication factor of the discretionary income to arrive at the business' value.

Capitalized Earning Approach: The capitalizing earning approach is based on the rate of return in earnings that the investor expects. For no risk investments, an investor would expect eight percent. Small businesses are usually expected to have a rate of return of 25 percent. Consequently, if your business has expected earnings of $50,000, its value might be estimated at $200,000 (200,000 * 0.25 = 50,000).

Cash Flow Method: This is determined by how much of a loan one could get based on the cash flow of the business. The cash flow is adjusted for amortization, depreciation, and equipment replacement. Then the loan amount is calculated with traditional loan business calculations. The amount of the loan is the value of the business.

Cost to Create Approach (Leapfrog Start-up): This is used when the buyer wants to buy an already functioning business to save start-up time and costs. The buyer estimates what it would have cost to start-up, minus what is missing in this business, plus a premium for the saved time.

Debt Assumption Method: This method usually gives the highest price. It is based on how much debt a business could have and still operate, using cash flow to pay the debt.

Discounted Cash Flow: The discounted cash flow is based on the assumption that a dollar received today is worth more than one received in the future. It discounts the business's projected earnings to adjust for real growth, inflation, and risk.

Excess Earning Method: This is similar to the Capitalized Earning Approach, but the return on assets is separated from other earnings which are interpreted as the "excess" earnings you generate. Usually return on assets is estimated from an industry average.

Multiple of Earnings: This is one of the most common methods used for valuing a business. In this method a multiple of the cash flow of the business is used to calculate its value.

Multiplier or Market Valuation: The market valuation uses an industry average sales figure from recent business sales in comparable businesses as a multiplier. For example, the industry multiplier for an ad agency might be .75, which is multiplied by annual gross sales to arrive at the value of the business.

Rule of Thumb Methods: These are quick and dirty methods based on industry averages that help to arrive at a starting point for the valuation. While not popular with financial analysts, this is an easy way to get a ballpark figure of what your business might be worth. Many industry organizations provide rule of thumb methods for businesses in their industry.

Tangible Assets (Balance Sheet) Method: This is often used for businesses that are losing money. The value of the business is based essentially on what the current assets of the business are worth.

Value of Specific Intangible Assets: This is useful when there are specific intangible assets that come with a business that are highly valuable to the buyer. For example, a customer base would be valuable to an insurance or advertising agency. The value of the business is based on how much it would have cost the buyer to generate this intangible asset.

Sale of an Incorporated Business

There are two ways to sell (or buy) a profitable incorporated business. You can do so through an asset sale or a share sale. Knowing which way is most advantageous to you can make a significant difference in the net proceeds if you are selling a business, or the net cost if you are buying one.

First, you could sell the shares of your company. Rather than selling the individual assets that your company owns, you sell your corporate shares. Once you sell your company's shares, the purchaser will automatically control the business operations and its assets.

Vendors often prefer to sell shares for several reasons:

1. A share sale is a simpler transaction. An asset sale would require that the vendor sell each individual asset, creating individual capital gains and losses on each item. Some of the income could also be recaptured capital cost allowance (tax depreciation), which must be fully included income.

2. After the assets have been sold, the vendor would need to wind up the empty company, incurring further legal and accounting fees.

3. A share sale creates capital gain income, which is only 50% taxable. Furthermore if a vendor's company meets the criteria for a qualified small business corporation he could be eligible to utilize his $750,000 lifetime capital gains exemption on the sale of his shares. This means that the vendor may not have to pay any income tax on the first $750,000 of gain from the business sale. This exemption is not available to a corporation that sells its assets.

4. Sometimes a business will have a history of operating losses. These losses can be used to offset the business's operating income of future years, only if the buyer purchases shares. If assets are purchased the buyer will not have access to these losses.

5. Finally, selling the land and building held by a corporation may also trigger the payment of land transfer taxes. If corporate shares were sold instead, the corporation would still own the land and no transfer taxes would apply.

Alternatively, you could sell the assets of your company. This would include selling the company's tangible assets, such as inventory, equipment, vehicles, furniture and fixtures, as well as the intangible assets, such as customer lists and goodwill that would be necessary for the prospective buyer to continue the business operations.

Purchasers generally prefer to buy the assets of the company rather than the shares for several reasons:

1. The purchaser can choose which assets of the company he wants to buy. If the company owns assets that are not vital for business operations, the buyer can exclude them from the purchase, reducing the overall purchase price.

2. Since most companies that are for sale have been in operation for some time, the assets have generally been depreciated for tax purposes. This means their tax value is often less than their market value. When the individual assets are purchased, it allows the buyer to "bump up" the tax value of those assets to their current market value. Since the assets then have a higher tax value, there are more deductions for capital cost allowance available to offset future income.

When you purchase a company's shares you also purchase the history of the company. Since a company is a separate legal entity, if there are any lawsuits, tax reassessments or other liabilities that relate to the period before you purchased the shares, the company, which you now own, will still be responsible for them.

If you purchase shares it is important that you become aware of any potential liabilities you may be purchasing inadvertently. In general with an asset purchase you are not responsible for any of the company's liabilities.

Strategies are available which provide the best of both approaches. The vendor can sell shares (and utilize the capital gains exemption) while the purchaser can minimize exposure to potential liabilities and be able to claim full depreciation on the fair market value of the assets. This strategy makes sense for larger deals in which the benefit from tax savings justifies the additional professional fees incurred.

Succession Planning:

Passing the Torch

After years of pouring your soul into building a successful business, it's probably hard to imagine your business without you holding the reins. But the day will come when you decide to step back and hand the responsibility for the day-today operations to someone else. What will become of your business when you retire? How does your business fit into your retirement plan? Even if you think you're years away from slowing down, the need to address these questions is a pressing one. Deciding how to leave your business is one of the major financial decisions of a business-owner's life.

Despite its importance, many business owners don't plan adequately and don't consider significant factors until they decide to leave. It's very likely your business is the most valuable asset you own. Perhaps you intend to pass it on to someone you trust, or maybe you'd be content to sell to the highest bidder. If you're not a sole proprietor, you might like your interest to be bought by your co-owner(s), partner(s), other shareholder(s), or certain key employees. You could then use the sale proceeds to fund your retirement or create an estate. Whatever your plan, you need to put an exit strategy in place today if you want to ensure that your business progresses as you want it to in the future.

There's also a good chance you'll want to pass it on to one or more members of your family. Succession planning, however, raises a number of difficult questions. If there is a family member who is both willing to take over the business and capable of running it, you're off to a good start. Next you have to decide how to finance the transfer. Will the new owner purchase an interest in the business – and if so, will he or she pay fair market value for it?

If you plan on leaving the shares to one person – for example, a child – are there enough other assets in your estate to leave to other children? If not, you might want to consider life insurance as a means of providing an inheritance to others. If you are considering leaving your business to siblings, proceed with care. Many families have suffered strained relationships after rifts have developed due to business questions or in situations in which one sibling feels he or she is contributing more than others. Also, if the plan calls for one sibling to take a more active role in the day-to-day operation of the business, will there be additional rewards for assuming extra responsibilities? You'll want to avoid a situation that leaves the active child to spend the rest of his or her life working for siblings.

If you haven't come to a decision yet, here are some options you might want to consider:

Convert your business into a source of retirement income

It's essential that you have a plan to convert the value of your business into cash when the time comes. There are three basic ways to do this.

Sell the business as a going concern to an outsider:
Labelling a business as a going concern means that you anticipate that your company will be able to function without resorting to liquidating assets or going out of business. While finding a potential buyer for a successful business is seldom difficult, finding the *right* buyer — someone who either has enough cash or has access to financing to be able to afford the purchase — is often more difficult. Selling a business is not straightforward. It is critical that you work with experienced, professional advisors to weigh the myriad of tax, legal, and accounting considerations.

Eventually you'll have to address number questions:

- If your business is incorporated, will you sell your shares or the assets?
- Can you use your capital gains exemption?
- Will you have to remove non-active investments from your business in order to qualify for the capital gains exemption?
- Will you have to extract operating assets, such as accounts receivable, to reduce the purchase price?

- Are you willing to accept a promissory note or mortgage to finance the sale?

Wind down your business:

If you are the biggest asset your business owns — in other words, if your business offers your professional services — you may not be able to sell it unless your client list has some value. If you're a professional whose expertise is in short supply, you may find that prospective purchasers are reluctant to pay for goodwill, since they'll be able to attract clients on their own relatively easily.

Preparing to close your doors for the final time can be difficult work. It might involve selling or disposing of remaining inventory; giving proper notice to landlords, creditors, and customers; and, in the case of a corporation, doing a certain amount of legal paperwork. Be prepared for the physical and emotional difficulty that accompanies the closing of a business. If your business is incorporated, the corporation may carry on while you slowly deplete its investments in a tax-efficient manner. But remember, maintaining a corporation requires ongoing administrative and legal expenses, so be sure to take these into account.

Pass on your business:

You may have relatives, co-owners, or key employees who want to take over your business when you're ready to retire. Facilitating this kind of transfer can be the most satisfying option, but it can also be the most complicated. It can be especially burdensome if other family members are excluded from the process. You'll need to establish a value for your business and be confident that your successor(s) will be successful without you. This might require involving these individuals in ownership concerns sooner rather than later. No matter how you choose to dispose of your business, it's critical that you make provisions for its disposition in your will. This is especially important if you plan on passing the business on to family members. You'll need to clearly delineate the means by which they will acquire the business. Will they purchase your share in it so that the proceeds go to your estate? Will they inherit ownership or a share in the business?

You also have to consider other members of your family. To avoid disputes you'll want to ensure that the distribution of your estate is equitable, so that all family members —including those who won't be brought into the business — are taken care of in some way.

Prepare for the tax burden

However you choose to wind-down your involvement, you must remember that any proceeds from a sale could be subject to income tax. By planning in advance, you can minimize the tax paid by you, your estate, or your heirs. Here are some examples you may want to consider:

1. The sale or deemed disposition of "qualified small business corporation shares" after death can qualify for a capital gains exemption of up to $750,000 for each shareholder. Ensure that your business qualifies.

2. A family trust or estate freeze could reduce taxes payable in the future and facilitate the transfer of ownership to family members.

3. You can plan your charitable bequests to maximize tax benefits. If transferring the business to family is your preference, consider life insurance proceeds that would cover the tax liability. Insurance can be a cost-effective way of financing the succession without saddling the business with the need to borrow money.

Ensure that your business shares receive the most favourable tax treatment

The shares you own in your corporation may not be eligible for the capital gains exemption. Ask your accountant if they qualify. If they don't, there may be steps you can take to "purify" the shares and ensure that they do qualify for this valuable exemption. In some cases, these measures must be in place 2 years before the sale of the business in order to be effective. Clearly, a failure to plan ahead can be costly.

Cap the tax liability on your business through an estate freeze

An estate freeze involves transferring ownership and the future growth of capital assets — usually to your children — now, rather than after your death. A failure to plan for business succession could leave your estate with a larger than necessary tax burden and can ultimately erode the value of your legacy. As a result of the freeze, you'll pay tax on capital gains accrued up to the date of transfer, and the new owners will be taxed on future gains. An estate freeze can be effective, but be careful not to implement a freeze too early or you could limit your own resources. An estate freeze can trigger immediate tax implications if not structured properly, so you should use tax professionals to ensure that it is structured properly.

Create a succession plan with the use of a family trust

Setting up a family trust at the time of an estate freeze appeals to many business owners because it allows them to plan the eventual transfer to their heirs and still maintain control. A trust involves an obligation on the part of the trustee to hold property for the benefit of the beneficiary. Trustees, which could include current owners, control the shares of the business in the best interest of the beneficiary for the period that the trust delineates. Trustees selected by the owners can exercise control for years after the death of the owner, as specified in the trust document.

The trust is a separate taxable entity, so any property owned by the trust would not form part of the owner's estate. Depending on where you reside, the establishment of a trust could also reduce probate fees down the road.

Enlist the help of a qualified professional

As you can see, there are countless factors to consider as you develop a strategy to leave your business. In order to get the best results, consult a qualified financial advisor. We can help with advice from a professional observer's point of view.

The Pillars of Succession Planning

Buy-sell agreement — These agreements establish the terms and conditions under which your share of the business or partnership will be acquired by your co-owners in the event of such contingencies as your death or disability.

Financial considerations — If you've chosen a successor, or signed a buy-sell agreement, you need to ensure that whoever will be taking over for you has the capital required to buy your interest. Insurance can ensure that the capital required in these situations is available when it's needed.

Legal documentation — Make sure your will and power of attorney coincide with the terms of the buy-sell agreement.

Managing the proceeds of your sale — Should you sell your business, you'll likely find yourself with a large sum of money in hand. The question is, how can those proceeds be invested to balance the need to minimize future tax concerns and still deliver respectable returns? A qualified financial planner can help you construct a properly diversified portfolio with the proceeds, based on your objectives and tolerance for risk.

Tim Chang is a Certified Financial Planner and Certified Management Accountant with 30 years of experience in Accounting, Taxation Consultancy, and Financial Planning .

He is an entrepreneur and owner of multiple businesses, including D!AL TAX Professional Corporation, an accounting & taxation practice since 1982. His mission in his work is to help people retire with dignity and to teach people how money works.

To find out how you can enjoy a dignified retirement visit:

http://www.dignifiedretirement.com